4.95

Sports and pastimes through the ages

Moss, Peter.

SPORTS AND PASTIMES THROUGH THE AGES

The seventeenth-century theatre

[See p. 117]

Sports and Pastimes through the Ages

by

PETER MOSS

Author of
"Our Own Homes through the Ages"
"Meals through the Ages"

Illustrated by
A. HOSSACK

Arco Publishing Company, Inc.

New York

To
Melanie
who loves all sports

First published 1963 *in the United States by*
ARCO PUBLISHING COMPANY, Inc.
480 Lexington Avenue, New York 17, N.Y.

© *Peter Moss* 1962

Library of Congress Catalog Card Number: 63-8625
ARCO Catalog Number: 1044

MADE IN GREAT BRITAIN

Contents

CHAPTER I

The Romans

THE sounds of Rome that echo down to us over the centuries are largely the serious noises of work. The tramp of the hobnailed legions; the clash of weapons as new lands are added to the Empire or subjects in revolt are crushed; the tap of masons' hammers as bridges, walls, and buildings are thrown up to linger through the ages; the chink of money as tax-collectors and merchants swarm in the wake of the conquering armies; and the steady drone of the orators, law-makers, and administrators—these are the voices that speak from our history books. Only rarely do we hear the faintest whisper of the roar from the arena or of the thunder of hooves from the circus: almost never do we hear the rattle of the dice-box, the slither of counters moved over the checkered board, or the quiet call of an indoor game. Yet perhaps of all the nations in history the Romans believed most firmly in the saying that all work and no play makes for dullness, and while it is true that the greatness of Rome rests on her soldiers, her lawyers, and her architects, if we find out how these men spent their leisure hours we shall understand more completely why their influence is felt so powerfully even to-day.

It is certain that never before the time of the Romans, or since, has the ordinary citizen enjoyed so much leisure, and when we think of our own week-ends and annual holidays we are amazed, horrified, or envious, according to our viewpoint. But the vast amount of free time was a gradual process, keeping in step with the growing might of the Latin people.

In the early centuries before Christ, when the Romans were a small, unimportant tribe, the people enjoyed the usual festivals connected with farming—midwinter, sowing-time, harvest—but as her armies began to push outward on their conquering way the anniversaries of certain victories were added to the list of holidays. Later still, days and weeks of games were ordered by the rulers to celebrate their birthdays or to gain favour with the people. By the second century A.D. there were at least six months a year when the citizen of Rome did little or no work, and for nearly three-quarters of this time he was provided with free entertainment by the Government or by wealthy citizens.

But of course this is only part of the story: behind this seeming paradise there looms the vast army of slaves, who, though on the whole well treated, never had a holiday, unless the few days at the feast of Saturnalia in December, when the household was turned topsy-turvy, could be counted. Only their constant work made it possible for the free men of Rome to enjoy such wonderful leisure. Then behind the slaves stood the Empire, reaching from Britain almost to India, and stretched to its limit to provide money, men, food, and animals for the conquerors' entertainment.

Although we are separated from the Romans by almost two thousand years, the average person of to-day would, with a few exceptions, find himself at home with most of their sports and pastimes, and the younger the time-traveller was, the happier he would be in the first centuries, for the youngest children of any age need few artificial amusements. The new world into which they have come is full of delights and surprises. Colour, movement, and sound are fun for the tiniest, and Roman babies were no exception. But if life with its noise and bustle

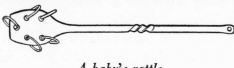

A baby's rattle

did begin to grow dull there were plenty of babies' rattles to keep the infant happy. The Romans called them *crepitacula*, and the word said aloud makes its own music. The more elaborate of these were made of bone or metal, and, apart from the fact that the violently bright colours of the Plastic Age would be missing, they would pass unnoticed amid scores of similar modern ones in any toyshop of our civilized world.

For a sleepier mood there were soft toys to cuddle. No doubt there were gaily coloured ducks, sheep, horses, lions, and elephants made of cloth and stuffed with feathers or wool, for miraculous though it may seem, a few rag dolls have been discovered. These, apart from their rather tattered appearance after eighteen centuries, seem to be identical with our own, even to the painted faces.

If the one-year-olds had no more than their rattles and stuffed animals to play with they could not complain, for at that age life itself is an adventure, and a cast-off cup, a piece of stick or stone, is as exciting a game as any that can be bought.

For the next six or twelve months of a baby's life the effort of learning to walk and the beginnings of speech make up a completely absorbing pastime, but once the novelty of these has worn off the demand for toys begins in real earnest. At first it is sufficient to be able to take one's self across the room, but soon the toddler longs for something he can push or pull on the journey, just to show how clever he really is.

The Roman child had a wide choice: all his favourite animals could be bought mounted on wheels, ready to be dragged at the end of a string or pushed by means of a stick fitting into the model's body. Naturally the finish of these toys and the material of which they were made depended on the family's wealth: a poorer child would have a clay creature, scarcely recognizable as an animal, mounted on wooden axles, with approximately round wooden or clay wheels. This would cost nothing apart from the time involved in its making, and if there was not a friendly potter to bake it in his furnace the hot Italian sun would oblige to make at least a temporary toy.

The more prosperous craftsman or farmer might buy for his family an animal sawn from a plank of wood and fixed to more or less true wooden wheels. Gaily painted, and possibly with a hair mane and tail fixed on, these would cause no comment at all in a nursery to-day, for toys like these still sell in thousands.

For the richer children there would be the elaborately carved figures in wood, bronze, glass, bone, or ivory, rolling on perfectly shaped metal wheels. Tigers, ducks, rabbits, and horses have all been found to show us how the young patrician amused himself. Some were harnessed to tiny metal or wooden carts or chariots so that the children, in imagination both driver and horse, could supply the city with foodstuffs, bring up the stores for the army, deliver a message for the emperor, or hurtle round the race-track.

As soon as a boy or girl became more agile, and could run quickly without getting feet in a tangle, the hoop phase began. Again, hoops could be as cheap or as expensive as one wished, for all that was really needed was a long, thin, supple stick such as a willow-wand, bent round into a circle, and tied at the join. Many of the hoops pictured in carvings seem to have been of this type, for the cord bindings are clearly visible. But perhaps, as in my own childhood, the wooden variety was considered fit only for girls, for boys are usually pictured with the noisy iron or bronze hoops which made a satisfying 'slurring' sound as they were driven over the pavements by a metal hook fitted to a wooden handle.

Sometimes small metal rings were fitted loosely to the rim and, by jingling as the hoop rolled along, added a 'chinking' to the slurring and clanking as the metal bounced on the uneven stone roads. For smaller children tiny bells were fastened to the inside of wooden hoops so that with their tinklings, clinkings, slurrings, and clankings—to say nothing of the flapping of racing feet and the cries of warning to pedestrians—the hoop season must have brought a musical touch to the steady general clangor of the Roman streets.

For most boys Hooping was a short-lived hobby, and soon joined the soft toys as a pastime it was better to forget as being a part of infancy.

A bronze hoop with rings But for many girls it was a lifelong passion, being a sport in which grown-up women could take part and enjoy physical exercise while still retaining a certain amount of dignity. Because of this hoops were extremely popular in the *Gymnasia* attached to the ladies' baths.

Somewhat akin to hoops, but requiring more skill, were tops. Perhaps in Rome, as now, their seasons ran together, or closely following, in the early spring when lengthening evenings and tingling air call for fairly active amusements. Roman tops were very similar to our pegtop—the type which looks like an old-fashioned beehive turned upside down, and which, unfortunately, is rarely seen nowadays. Wood was no doubt the commonest material, but clay and ivory tops have been discovered, some beautifully decorated with flowers and leaves on the top and round the upper edges. A two-thonged whip was used, and if the streets became too crowded for the sport, which could not be enjoyed to its full in the crush of the market-place, there were always the open spaces in the public parks, such as the Campus Martius, reserved for games.

At an early age too the Roman was introduced to ball games, a pastime which, for a boy at least, kept his interest right through life until rheumatism or old age made him completely inactive. The balls for fumbling, unskilled, tiny hands would be large and brightly coloured, made of cloth, and stuffed, like the rag animals, with soft material. The *follis*, a leather-covered ball which older boys and men used in a game similar to our Handball, contained a blown-up animal bladder in a similar fashion to our footballs and netballs, and it is possible that some of the large cloth balls were inflated in the same way for lightness. Blown up by the mouth only, they would not have been as 'hard' as ours, and because of their flabbiness they would have been poor bouncers.

As the children became older and more used to handling balls they would pass to other smaller types, covered with cloth or sewn leather, stuffed with sand, seeds, or feathers. There may have been solid wooden balls, but strangely enough the idea of a bat or racquet does not seem to have occurred to the Romans, so that all of their ball games were played with the hands only.

Probably the most popular of the children's games was one called *Trigon*, which, as its name implies, was played by three people.

The players stood in the form of a triangle, the distance between them varying with their age and skill. Each was armed with a small ball of wood or leather about the size of our tennis-ball, and on the word 'Go' the balls would be tossed from one to the other. There was no definite order in the throwing, for the object of the game was to make one of the players drop his catch. The ball could be caught and rethrown, punched back with the fist, or glanced aside with the hand to the third member so that the pace could be furious. The great skill was to throw so that one player had to catch balls from each of the other two and throw his own at the same time—a feat demanding at least three hands. The winner was the player who had the fewest 'drops' after a given time. To speed up the game, and to keep the throwing running smoothly, richer children, and adults, who were particularly fond of this sport before the baths, were attended by slaves with a fresh supply of balls to hand to their masters whenever a catch was dropped.

There were more complicated and organized team games with balls, but these were most probably played by older children and men. Of these, *Paganica* and *Harpastum* are two names that have come down to us, but the actual rules of play of both have been lost. *Harpastum* seems to have been played by two teams on a rectangular pitch divided across the middle. We know the position of only one player—the middleman—who bore the brunt of the attack, for we are told he could be attacked and wrestled with. Possibly the object of the game was to pass the ball from man to man and ground it behind the opponents' baseline, rather in the fashion of Rugby Football.

Of *Paganica* we know even less, but it is thought that the two teams lined up behind their baselines and rushed for the ball, which had been placed in mid-field, on the signal to begin. Again there seems to have been passing from hand to hand and tackling, though the method of scoring is unknown. There were teams of professional ball players who toured the country playing matches in arenas and charging for their displays rather like modern footballers and cricketers. In the army too there were most probably matches between companies and perhaps even legions, for it seems unlikely that the officers would let such a wonderful opportunity for keeping their men fit and relieving the monotony of months of guard duty pass by.

There is little doubt that there must have been scores of other catching-and-throwing games, although the names of only a few have been recorded.

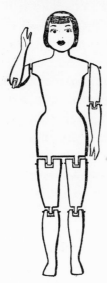

A jointed doll

While the growing boy turned more and more from his toys to his ball games the girls prepared to be good wives and mothers with their dolls. These too varied widely in cost and construction, but, as now, most of them were 'girl' dolls. A few have been found carved as if fully dressed, but the great majority are naked. The reason is obvious: three-quarters of the fun of doll games is the dressing and undressing, and 'girl' figures are much more attractive to clothe than 'boys.'

The crudest dolls of all were the clay figures fashioned by the children themselves, and whose arms and legs were little more than lines scratched in the lump of mud. A scrap of discarded cloth provided a complete wardrobe, and imagination supplied the missing hair and features. At the other extreme were the life-like dolls of wood or ivory with shaped bodies and legs, jointed limbs, and painted features. Normally, the arms and legs were jointed at the shoulders and thighs only, but some had further movement at the knee and elbow. Strangely enough, movable heads do not seem to have occurred to the Romans, so that whatever life-like attitudes the limbs may have assumed, the doll gazed ever forward in a stiff-necked glare.

We find references to sets of dolls' clothing, and it is reasonable to suppose that tiny sandals were included. Miniature furniture and kitchen equipment, tiny combs and cosmetic jars, found by archeologists, all show that the dolls of the first centuries A.D. had quite a high standard of life,

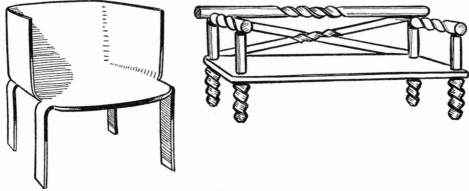

Lead doll's furniture

and it is not beyond the bounds of possibility that those belonging to the nobler homes had their own tiny houses, as have their twentieth-century counterparts.

There may have been some too poor even for the cheapest toy, but if these children could run together in the streets or parks there were plenty of games that demanded no equipment at all. When the violent chasing, climbing, and horseplay had taken the edge from their energy there were many round games which could be played quietly. *Basilinda*, for example, was probably a kind of O'Grady Says, for we know that one person was king and the others were subjects obeying his commands. Nero, we read, played this as a child, and it is not hard to guess which part he took.

With a little imagination and the litter and jumble of Rome there need never have been a dull moment for the street urchin. A baulk of timber from one of the many ruined blocks of flats would make a seesaw: a rope snatched from the quayside could be used for the great game of Swinging. Hopscotch squares and mazes could be scratched on the roadways, and if all else failed there was the never-ending game of watching the city itself.

But even children find the heat of an Italian summer afternoon too much for vigorous games, so that as the midday sun blistered down the Roman boys and girls crept into the coolness of their own homes, if they were wealthy enough, or into the shade of one of the great public buildings, within sound of a splashing fountain, if they lived in the poorer parts of the city. Even then there was no shortage of peaceful games to pass the drowsy hours until the cool of evening woke the city to bustling life again.

The girls had their dolls, of course, which are as good out of doors as in, or they could join the boys in one of the many games played with nuts. Nuts could be used as marbles—either the game in which the marble is thrown into a hole or circle in the road or the one in which the object is to hit the opponent's piece. They could be used for the game of Piling, rather like the modern matchstick-stacking, in which the person who could make a pyramid with the most nuts without the whole heap collapsing was the winner. If everything else had been exhausted there were the simple gambling games which involved guessing which hand held the nut or whether an odd or even number was contained in the clenched fist. So great a part did nuts take in the games of childhood that the slang expression in Rome for growing up was "to leave your nuts."

Fivestones, or Knucklebones, was always popular as a 'quiet' game with both children and adults—especially women. Real knucklebones—the bones from the foot of a cloven-hoofed animal—were best, naturally, but if these could not be obtained pebbles, cherry-stones, or the universal nuts could be tossed in the air to be caught alternately on the back and the palm of the hand. Any which dropped had to be snatched up from the ground while the others were in the air between catches. Some of the bones which have been discovered are beautifully decorated, and even inlaid with amber and precious stones. Some, obviously grown-ups' sets, were made of bronze, glass, or alabaster, shaped as the natural bones. Judging by the number of knucklebones found, both real and artificial, not only must the Romans have been extraordinarily fond of the game, but also remarkably careless with their pieces.

But of all the sitting-down games for a small group, there is no doubt that Dicing and *Micare* were by far the most popular. Both could be played equally well indoors or out, and both were an excuse for gambling. Betting was illegal except at the feast of Saturnalia and for games involving physical skill, such as Chariot-racing, but most people either ignored the law or found a way round it. *Micare* was the simpler game, demanding no equipment other than the fingers of one hand. The players paired off, each with his right hand behind his back, and at a pre-arranged signal—perhaps a nod from one of them—both shot out their hands with a number of fingers raised. At the same instant each called out what he thought the total of fingers on the two hands would be, and

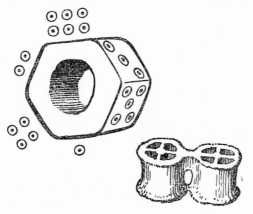

Dice and Knucklebones

if neither guessed correctly the process was repeated. Although this sounds very childish, it can involve quite a deal of shrewd thinking and study of one's opponent's tactics—some people usually follow three or four one-or-two-finger showings with a 'five,' whereas others tend to show one, two, three, four, and five in successive attempts. But allowing for the subtle craft, it does seem a game invented specially for cheats and arguers, and the proverb which a Roman used when commenting on a person's honesty was "You can play *Micare* with him in the dark."

Gambling with dice was universal: the humblest slave and the greatest emperor alike played it, the only difference being that the slave would have less time for the sport and his bets would be very much lower. There were dice of every shape, size, and material: wooden, clay, bone ivory, glass, alabaster, jade, iron, and precious metal dice have been discovered, ranging in size from three-sixteenths of an inch to two or more inches long. Most were numbered from 1 to 6, but brick-shaped dice often had only 1, 3, 4, and 6, while still others had no numbers but letters. The majority were naturally cube-shaped, but some unusual people delighted in rectangular, hexagonal, lozenge-shaped, and even twenty-four-sided ones. The most delightful dice of all, however, were those in the shape of a pin-man seated with his legs stretched out in front at an angle, and his hands on his hips. These figures of silver or bronze were so made that they could fall in six positions—on the back (5 showing on the stomach), on the face (6 showing on the back), on the left side (3), on the right side (2), sitting upright (1 on the crown of the head), and upside down (4 showing on the seat). It is a pity that some enterprising manufacturer does not make them to-day.

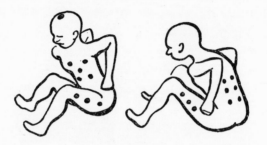

Mannikin dice

In one aspect of dice-throwing the Romans were ahead of the twentieth century: we all know of certain boys and girls who, when they need a particular number to win a game, place the dice in the shaker so that if the cup is turned over quickly the required figure appears. The Romans suffered from such people too, and to foil their schemes the inside of the shaker was often ridged. These projections caught in the dice as it dropped, turned it over, and ensured a fair throw every time.

If the Italian summers were hot it is also true that the winters could be cold and damp, so that a great deal of time had to be spent indoors. It is here that the modern child has a great advantage over the boys and girls of two thousand years ago, for the indoor games of Rome were very limited.

For those who could read and lived in a sufficiently large town there were 'books'—long, rolled sheets of parchment which could be borrowed from the public library. Except to a very unusual boy or girl, the histories, biographies, poems, and speeches which were the literature of the day were very dull stuff, and few read them from choice. If, however, one was inclined to be studious there were sets of bone or ivory letters with which words could be built and spellings learnt. Again, if one's mind ran on these lines there were word-squares to be made up, such as the famous one found scratched on a tile near Reading which reads the same in four directions:

S	A	T	O	R	(a sower)
A	R	E	P	O	(a man's name)
T	E	N	E	T	(he holds)
O	P	E	R	A	(works, deeds)
R	O	T	A	S	(wheels)

The words, of course, have no meaning as a sentence.

But the child who was taught to read and write probably had quite enough of this during lesson-time with his tutor, and turned to more entertaining pastimes when he was free to choose.

For the lucky boy there might be a 'whirler'—a metal disc with two small holes through which a cord passed. The ends of the cord were joined, and slipped over the hands. By alternately pulling and loosening the string, the disc whirred round at a satisfying, if somewhat dangerous, speed. There were also yo-yos made of metal, but like the whirlers they were actually Greek, and probably rarely found in Rome except when brought by a returning traveller.

In a nation so proud of its army, toy soldiers were bound to be inevitable. There were rough clay ones, lead ones, and beautifully carved ones in harder metals. There were foot-soldiers, cavalry, supply wagons, pack-horses and chariots, and, no doubt, forts. In a land where most men had had some experience of the army and of war, no doubt the Roman fathers' attitude to their sons' toy armies was very similar to that which modern fathers have towards their sons' toy train sets. There must have been many unsoldierly tears when young Marcus, having manoeuvred his second legion into a winning position, suddenly found the high command whisked from his hands by Father.

For the occasions when the noise of battle could not be permitted in the dining-room there were board games, of which only two have come down to us by name, and of these the actual details of play are very vague. The first, *Duodecim Scripta*, or Twelve Lines, was a game for two people, rather like Backgammon, and was played on a board divided into three columns of thirteen squares each. The men, fifteen black and fifteen white, moved under the throws of three dice up one row, down the centre, and back up the third, all the while subject to certain hazards

B

and to capture by the opposing side. The winner was the first person to work all of his men safely to the end of the course.

The other game, the Game of Soldiers, or, as it was sometimes called, the Game of Robbers, was also for two players, and bore some resemblance to Chess, though it was much more simple. Played on a checkered board whose number of squares seems uncertain, it had two types of 'men'—officers and soldiers. It is possible that the 'soldiers' moved forward one square at a time, the 'officers' moved diagonally, and to make a capture the 'piece' had to be sandwiched between two of the 'enemy's' men. The winner was obviously the person who captured the whole of his opponent's force or forced him into a position from which he could not move.

There must have been many other games of similar type for almost every Roman excavation reveals large numbers of counters of metal, bone, or stone, often decorated with dots. Clay tiles are constantly being unearthed too, with rough scratchings on them, sometimes of plain check patterns, and at other times with diagonal lines superimposed on the squares, but we have no idea how these games were played.

Perhaps the most intriguing indoor game of all is one which was played with rectangular slips of bone, about two inches long and half an inch wide, inscribed on one side with a number, and on the other with a word. The numbers run from 1 to 25, with 30 and 60 in addition, and while the lower ones bear on the reverse rather insulting words—*nugator* (trifler), *stumacose* (bad-tempered), *malest* (bad luck), and *fur* (thief)— the higher ones had congratulatory words—*felix* (happy), and *benigne* (lucky). Apart from the bare fragments, we have no details of the game at all, but it must have been a jolly one, and most suitable for children.

The last indoor amusement, again one imported from Greece, was more popular with adults—for whom there was no excuse—than with children. The only apology that can be offered is that *Cottabus*, as the game was called, was normally played after a meal, when the freely passing wine had taken the edge from the sense of decency. A mark would be fixed on the ceiling or floor by one of the company, usually the master of ceremonies, and each of the diners as he reached the bottom of his glass of wine would hurl the dregs at the mark. At other times a specially designed bowl on a stand was placed at some distance from the table, and the diners would try to throw the last few drops of their drink into this without splashing. One can only hope that the majority of children were asleep before this performance began.

So the Roman children grew into their teens, the girls keeping their hoops and knucklebones, and the boys their balls and dice. The girls usually kept their dolls, too, until they married, when the little wooden figures were dedicated on the altars of Venus or the household gods. Unlike the Greek youths, the Romans did not take kindly to any form of athletics except the throwing of the discus, and passed straight into the passive, rather than the active, stage of entertainment.

The four great adult amusements of the Roman world covered the whole range of taste: the theatre at its best was uplifting or amusing; the circus with its hurtling chariots provided the thrilling excitement of a modern horserace, a racing-car duel, and a wall-of-death rider all in one; the arena with its host of gladiators and wild beasts brought to the surface that cruelty and blood-lust that lay just beneath the skin of so many Romans; and the baths provided every aspect of entertainment the cultured man could desire.

Unlike the pastimes already mentioned, which could be played at any time, and the baths which were available every day, the theatre, circus, and arena were open only during the days and weeks of the great games such as the Roman Games (September 4–19), the People's Games (November 4–17), Games of the Goddess Flora (April 28–May 3), Caesar's Victory Games (July 20–30), and many others, and even then not all three amusements were running at once. The cost of the sports was borne either by the Government or by a wealthy noble or emperor anxious to increase his popularity, so that admission was free, enabling every one except slaves to attend.

The best of the public entertainments, the theatre, never achieved the popularity of the others, and towards the end of the Roman period was sadly neglected, particularly when the classical tragedies or comedies were being played. The theatre building itself was a huge open-roofed semicircle, the largest being 160 yards in diameter and seating about twenty-five thousand people, or twelve times as many as a large modern opera house. The stage was a long shallow platform, usually roofed, on the straight side of the building, and possessed permanent scenery in the form of a street of houses with three doors, windows, and pillars. Before the performance began this stage was screened by means of a curtain which rolled downward into a slot at the front, as opposed to the modern practice in which the curtains move upward.

Immediately in front of the stage was a level semicircular area known as the orchestra which was normally empty, but which may have been filled with seats on special occasions. Running round the orchestra, one above the other, were the tiers of seats of wood or stone, or perhaps, in very remote districts, of earth. The first rows of these—that is, those nearest to the stage—were reserved for the nobility, and there was usually a railed-in box—or perhaps two—at the level of the lowest seats for the giver of the show and for the emperor or the senior official present.

Although the farthest seats were up to eighty yards from the stage, the buildings were so skilfully constructed that the sound carried perfectly. But sight is a different matter, and without opera glasses, which of course had not been invented, it was impossible to distinguish details such as actors' features clearly at such a distance. To overcome this difficulty, and so that all of the spectators could follow the play, each character on the stage had its traditional style of dress, in a particular colour, and a mask. An old man, for example, always wore a white robe; a young one, a multicoloured robe. Women, always played by men in serious drama, wore yellow clothes and, to distinguish them further, had white masks instead of the men's brown ones.

In case both mask- and dress-colouring were not enough, the different characters passed through different doors when making exits and entrances: gods and princes used the doorway in the centre of the stage, women and slaves the one on the left, and the other characters the one on the right.

The tragedies were stories of the gods and ancient heroes, usually adapted from the Greek and, to modern ears, rather dull. There were long speeches in which little action took place, and to make the actors representing the gods seem so much more magnificent than ordinary mortals they wore shoes with soles a foot thick, padded themselves out to keep their figures in proportion, and even piled their hair on top of their heads to add greater height. Like some of the more obscure medieval plays occasionally seen to-day, the tragedies appealed to only a very few people, the majority finding complicated plots which demanded a deep knowledge of the family history of the gods far too difficult to understand and enjoy. Because of this the tragedy in its original form soon disappeared from the stage.

The theatre

The comedies were more popular for a time, and make very amusing reading even to-day. They are usually lighthearted stories of gay young men-about-town outwitting a stern and miserly father with the aid of a scheming slave. As in the tragedies, masks and traditional robes were used to make the characters more easily identifiable, yet even this did not satisfy the Roman audiences for long. Seeking ever something lighter and more exciting, the theatregoers forced the comic plays to change into the pantomime.

There had always in the more serious drama been songs or musical interludes between the acts, and these gradually assumed a more and more important part of the performance until the old pieces had changed into what we should call musical comedy—short snatches of the old dialogue joining up the songs and dances. The chief singer became increasingly important until instead of being quite a minor performer he dominated the whole entertainment. The pantomime, as he was called, danced, sang, mimed, and acted one character after another until it became almost a one-man show. It is true there were other stock characters such as the hunchback and the fool, but these were there only to 'feed' the pantomime with material, and to be the butt of his jokes and slapstick. There is no doubt that the pantomimes, although usually men of very low birth, were brilliantly gifted, but their trade was filthy, for their shows played on the worst emotions of cruelty and nastiness in all their forms.

Yet, even so, the pantomime was not the lowest level to which the Roman theatre sank: in the very depths of horror, and for this reason the most popular, was the mime. Here the last shreds of connexion with serious drama were cast aside, for the actors dressed, not in masks and costumes, but in the ordinary clothes of the street, and women, the very lowest, performed on the stage. The mimes were portrayals of the very worst scenes from life—crime, wickedness, and vice in all its aspects. It is sufficient to say that if a play called for a death, as it usually did, the players were often given a condemned criminal to torture or burn alive in front of the audience. It seems strange that the Romans, so cultured in so many respects, could permit and even encourage such scenes of depravity as could be witnessed in the later days of the theatre.

While discussing the black side of the Roman nature one cannot, however much one would like to do so, avoid the amphitheatre, the horror of which still catches the breath after eighteen centuries.

Actors in a tragedy

Wherever the Romans settled and made a reasonably sized community the first luxury they permitted themselves would be the baths: the next would most probably be an arena. In the distant provinces this would be no more than a hollow in the ground with wooden seats provided on the mounds of excavated earth, but in the capital the most famous amphitheatre of them all, the Colosseum, still rears its huge bulk, a quarter of a mile round, to astound us.

The actual arena, two hundred and eighty-one feet long and one hundred and seventy-seven feet wide, or the size of a small football-pitch, was surrounded by a fifteen-foot wall for safety's sake: above this barrier the seats, fifty thousand of them, ran round in concentric tiers, the upper-most being almost one hundred and eighty feet above the ground. Here, on the sand covering the boarded floor, gladiators hacked each other to pieces; men, armed and unarmed, fought every strange and savage animal the Empire could capture, and packs of wild beasts tore one another apart for the entertainment of the mob.

The gladiators, who were recruited from slaves, prisoners-of-war, convicted prisoners, or sometimes penniless young noblemen, lived and trained in barracks like soldiers. Their lives were alternating terror and luxury, for those who survived were well paid, a famous fighter with many victories to his credit receiving even more than a well-known actor.

There were many styles of armour and equipment for the fighters, most of whom were on foot, but occasionally there were combats on horseback or in chariots. Some were heavily armed, some lightly, but two types, *retiarius* and *secutor*, seem to have caught the public imagination. *Secutor* wore a helmet, breastplate, and leg-guard, and was armed with a short sword and shield; *retiarius* wore little or no protection, and was equipped with a net in which to catch his adversary and a trident to give the death-blow. Perhaps the styles of fighting which these represented— the heavily-armed, solid cut-and-slash of *secutor* contrasted with the speedy footwork and lightning dart of *retiarius*—appealed as much to Roman audiences as does a similar contrast in a modern boxing-ring.

Imagine a day of gladiatorial games: the wooden posts on the topmost parapet of the amphitheatre have been erected to enable the canvas screens to be pulled over to temper the heat of the sun. Slaves have paraded up and down the gangways, spraying the air with saffron-scented water to cool down the atmosphere while the thousands of inflamed spectators thrill with a dreadful excitement as they watch the doomed men march round the arena to raise their traditional salute to the emperor—"We who are about to die salute thee, O Caesar." There is a muttering as the preliminary sham battle with wooden weapons begins, and then an expectant silence as the gladiators' managers examine the real weapons to reject the blunt ones. The tumult breaks forth as the first contest begins: lots have been drawn for opponents, and the victims walk to the centre, each fully aware that only by the grace of the gods will he return at the end of the contest. Each gives an apprehensive look towards the slaves dangling ropes and hooks at the entrance to the tunnel where the dead are dragged, and then the grim battle is joined.

Sometimes a contest was of one man against another; sometimes small armies locked in combat. At other times there was a fight without remission in which the winner of the first duel was immediately attacked by a third, fresh gladiator who in his turn was set upon by a fourth. But whatever the particular conflict, the dreadful scenes continued, hour after hour, day after day, for there was no satisfying the blood-lust of the mob.

The climax of a particular event occurred when one of the fighters fell or surrendered. The actual decision whether the vanquished opponent should be slaughtered rested with the victorious gladiator who, in order to gain favour with the emperor or senior official present, usually appealed to the royal box for a decision. The emperor, for much the same reason as the gladiator, normally passed the final judgment to the crowd who did not hesitate to give the thumbs-up signal if they thought the unfortunate man merited death. On the other hand, the mob could recognize a good performance, and the thumbs-down sign allowed the wretch to live to endure another day of hope, despair, and terror.

Occasionally a gladiator put up such a good fight that the emperor awarded him a wooden sword, which meant that he was freed from any more service in the arena and could become a free citizen. But so deeply was slaughter rooted in many of the fighters' minds that after a period of liberty they returned voluntarily to the ranks of the killers for fame, or money, or merely for the love of battle.

Constantly the rabble sought new excitements: men against beasts, beasts against other beasts, and sometimes a *naumachia*. For this most spectacular of gladiatorial battles either a special pool or artificial lake was built, or the normal arena was flooded with water from a near-by river. When the water was sufficiently deep iron-beaked warships manned by gladiators hurled themselves across it, driven by creaking oars, to offer something novel in the way of killing to the maddened spectators.

But black though the general picture of the amphitheatre is, there were brighter moments, and occasionally in the times of the more enlightened emperors even the smallest child could have watched quite happily. Such performances were very similar to our circuses: companies of cavalry and highly drilled foot-soldiers gave displays of military skills and riding, and wild animals performed tricks that showed many months of skilful training. Once, for example, elephants wrote the emperor's name in the sand with their trunks; monkeys rode on tigers' backs; cranes gave a dancing display; and lions carried their trainers round the arena in their mouths.

Exhibitions of hunting were given, as when two unarmed Egyptians captured alive a number of crocodiles for the benefit of the thousands peering down at the unfamiliar creatures. In the provinces, particularly in Britain and Gaul, Cockfighting was extremely popular, and this, though undoubtedly cruel, did divert men's minds from the slaughter of one another.

Normally, however, these harmless acts were given as interludes between the bloodthirsty murder that was the main business of the amphitheatre. The arenas, from the magnificent buildings in the capital to the humble pits on the fringe of the Empire, must remain for ever a deep blot on the name of Rome.

The circus, or racing-track, fought with the amphitheatre for the leading place in popularity with the people. It was without doubt extremely thrilling, and what was very important to the gambling-mad Romans, as a sport demanding physical skill it was free from the general ban on betting. The race was very dangerous, but probably not more so than our modern Motor-racing, and death was not inevitable as it was in the arena.

The Circus Maximus, the most famous of all the tracks, was a huge building six hundred and ninety-four yards long and one hundred and sixty-four yards wide, with the usual tiers of seating surrounding a rectangular track with semicircular ends. Estimates of its capacity range from sixty thousand to a quarter of a million, but it seems likely that it

The amphitheatre

could accommodate about one hundred thousand spectators in reasonable comfort. The immense size, together with the stalls, shops, and brightly coloured toilets made the Circus Maximus one of the wonders of the Roman world. Outside the capital the circuses were naturally much more simple, consisting of the track with perhaps an earth bank surrounding it, but, elaborate or primitive, they were all basically the same.

Down the centre of the sanded running-track ran a low broad wall known as the spine, and this served to divide the area into two parts. The ends of the spine, which were the turning-points, were marked by pillars so that the exact spot when the teams had to be dragged round, sliding and staggering, to gallop down the opposite side, could be clearly seen by the drivers in the heat of the race. The wall itself was decorated with statues and altars and, most important of all, with the lap-recorders. These consisted of stands holding seven large wooden 'eggs'—rather like a coconut on a stick. One of these was removed each lap to enable spectators to follow exactly the progress of the race. Sometimes the lap-recorders consisted of seven dolphins standing on their heads. One of these was turned round each time the whole field had galloped past.

The chariots themselves were light two-wheeled vehicles, sometimes merely a wooden framework filled in with leather thonging. More usually, however, they were rather more substantial, if only to withstand the severe strains imposed on them during a race. They could be drawn by two, three, four, six, or even eight horses, but the *quadriga*, or four-horse team, was by far the most popular.

Like successful gladiators or actors the drivers could gain great wealth and fame, but many met an early death in the terrible crashes on the course: Scorpus, one of the most famous charioteers, won over two thousand races before he died beneath the pounding hooves. Each driver wore a tunic the same colour as his chariot—red, green, blue, or white—for these were the colours of the factions who owned and trained the teams.

Those of you who live in cities that have two football-teams in the same league will know how high words and fights can develop between rival followers: imagine a city in which every person supported one of the four 'colours' and was a hundred more times fanatical in his devotion to his 'team' than we are to-day. Then you will get some idea of how the Roman world was split: fights were normal at race-meetings, bloodshed common, and frequently the army had to be called in to prevent whole-

The circus

sale slaughter of one section of the community by the angry supporters of a rival party.

The faction bitterness continued all the year round, but at the games at which Chariot-racing was to take place it must have risen to fever pitch. Whipped to a frenzy by their loyalties—and by the bets they had made—the crowd could scarcely contain themselves during the preliminaries of the meeting. As the emperor or consul, the priests and other officials, made their ceremonial entry and tour of the course, the spectators' minds were focused on the moment when the white cloth would drop from the royal box as a signal for the start of the sports.

The doors of the stables at the end of the track would fly open, and the chariots, usually four at a time, one for each colour, would move up to the white line which represented the starting-point. Each driver would be tensed, knowing well that fortune or perhaps death waited him in the next seven laps. The reins were knotted round his waist and held lightly in his left hand; his dagger was loose in its sheath in case it was needed to cut the harness in an accident, and his whip was poised for the first slash. He tensed himself, waiting for the trumpet that would send him hurtling round two miles of sliding sand and fourteen terrible hairpin corners.

The race was always run in an anticlockwise direction, and it was at the turns that it was usually won or lost. Here, especially on the first lap when the chariots were more or less bunched together, the skill and courage of the men were most needed: too sharp a turn would probably overturn the vehicle, wrecking at least one other competitor in a fury of plunging hooves, while too wide a turn would lose many yards. Iron resolution, a giant's strength, lightning reaction, and extraordinary skill were demanded, and the more of each quality there was the greater was the thrill for the hoarse, cheering thousands peering through the clouds of dust and sand.

One by one the 'eggs' would be removed, or one by one the dolphins turned. Then would come the jockeying thunder round the last bend and the fight up the finishing straight to cross the winning-line opposite the royal box amid the roars of joy or despair.

Up to twenty-four races a day were run, and the main events were sometimes varied by 'stunts' in the intervals. There might be displays of riding, comic races by camel-drawn chariots, and, most popular of all, the *Desultores*. These were races in which pairs of horses loosely fastened

The gymnasium

together galloped round the track guided by jockeys who at full speed leapt from one horse to another. In short, without the bitterness of the faction quarrels and perhaps with some safety precautions, the Roman circus would be enjoyed by millions of people to-day if it were revived.

Perhaps the greatest of all the entertainments of the Romans has been left till last: the baths. It was more than an amusement—it was a way of life that sums up all that was best in the great Empire. A tiny town in that most outlandish of all provinces, Britain, would have no theatre, no arena, and no circus, but it would indeed be a poor settlement that did not boast a bath-house of some sort. Although the pleasures that a rude *Thermae* on the wild moors near Hadrian's Wall could offer would be very different from those of one of the great baths at Rome, the spirit was the same.

Like the great entertainments, the baths were usually free, or charged such a low admission fee that even the poorest could afford their pleasures. Unlike the theatre, circus, and amphitheatre where the lower rows of seats were reserved for the noble families, the baths offered no social barriers, so that we have left us a delightful description of a conversation between an emperor and one of his old soldiers, both perspiring in the hot-rooms.

Basically, the *Thermae* consisted of a room heated to a high temperature by hot air passing under the floor where the bather sweated freely, and a second room, usually containing a cold-water pool, where the bather cooled down. To these were added as many luxuries as circumstances demanded or money allowed, but a normally well-equipped establishment would have a changing-room, a cold-room (*frigidarium*) with a cold plunge, a warm-room (*tepidarium*), a hot-room (*calidarium*) containing a bath of hot water, and finally, perhaps, a very hot dry-heat room (*laconicum*) where the temperature was scarcely bearable. The hot air from the hypocaust furnace passed first under the hot dry-room, then under the hot- and warm-rooms, and often ended up when most of the heat had gone by slightly warming the changing-room.

Children were usually admitted free even if there was a small charge for adults, and one hopes they took advantage of the concession, for it was as pleasant a way of passing an afternoon as the ancient world could devise. Although there was no set routine, and the delights could be sampled in any order, a bather might stick to the following fairly common plan.

The baths: scraping in the warm-room

Arriving at the baths soon after it had opened at midday, for by evening the hot-room really lived up to its name, our bather and his friends would strip in the changing-room or perhaps remove only their outdoor clothes, depending on the next step. Accompanied by a slave carrying the equipment needed, they would pass to the *gymnasium* where every form of violent exercise could be seen in progress: some played *Trigon* or other ball games, some ran or leapt, some skipped or swung dumb-bells; others lunged at, and stabbed, a scarred wooden post with swords, while the most energetic, stark naked and well greased, wrestled in pairs. The elderly might even trundle a hoop round the outside of the hurly-burly of the more active ones.

This exercise served to start the perspiration flowing, and when feeling hot and exhausted the bathers moved to the warm-room where they began to sweat in real earnest. When the trickles had begun to run freely they moved to the hot-room, where they sprinkled themselves with hot water from the basin, or, if they felt like Spartan methods, to the hot dry-room, where the terrific heat opened every pore in the body.

When the bathers had had as much of the hot-rooms as they wanted— or could stand, in many cases—they moved back to the warm-room for scraping, towelling, massage, and perfuming. If they had not brought their own slaves for the purpose they could hire one of the attendants in the *tepidarium*, for even if towelling and perfuming could be managed, scraping and massage are tasks which one cannot very satisfactorily perform for oneself.

The *strigilis* which was used for scraping off the sweat and sprinkled water was a blunt, knife-like instrument, and was often found as part of a toilet-set comprising tweezers for removing hairs, nail-cleaners and file, and ointment spoon. To judge from accounts written at the time, the slaves in charge of massage and sweat-scraping showed no mercy, particularly when hair-plucking was included in the toilet routine, but when the painful part had been completed there was the joy of being anointed with sweet-smelling oils and creams from long-necked flasks.

Our bathers, clean, sleek, and feeling wonderfully light, would pass into the *frigidarium* for a plunge in the cold pool to close the pores and to add a final ringing glow of health to their bodies. In the pool itself they could swim or merely wallow, seated on the underwater steps, talking to friends.

Dried and dressed again, there were all the delights of cultured Rome

awaiting if the baths were large enough. There was the lounge in which
to discuss politics, the races, or the latest prices of corn; there was the
promenade with the latest collection of statues, busts, and paintings on
show and begging to be criticized; there was the corner where the aspiring
author or poet read aloud his latest work; there were the stalls of sweet-
meats which undid all the good that had been done in the hot-room; and
finally, for the really keen and energetic, there was the *gymnasium* again.

But while the capital revelled, the twinkling lights of civilization on
the edges of the Empire were, by the end of the fourth century, beginning
to fade as the barbarians swept through the defences. Nearer and nearer
to the centre came the darkness, but in Rome itself the light burned more
brightly for a while, for in 404 A.D. the horrors of the amphitheatre were
abolished by law. Yet the circus and the baths had but a short reign of
supremacy before they too vanished, and only now, after nearly sixteen
centuries, can the world see again within measurable distance such a
standard of relaxation for its people.

CHAPTER II

The Saxons

LONG before the last legions left Britain in a vain attempt to save their own land Roman civilization had been slowly dying in this outermost island of the Empire. By the time the Angles and Saxons made their invasions the days of the great games had gone and were nothing but a memory handed down from father to son. The earth amphitheatres outside the almost derelict towns were overgrown by brambles, and apart from an occasional cockfight were perhaps never used. The few wooden or stone theatres had long been torn to the foundations for fuel or building material, and while here and there in the villas that remained a few kept up the habit of bathing, most of the public baths in the towns were already in ruins.

The savage invaders certainly did not bother to revive the lost amusements even if they had known of them, for unlike the pleasure-loving Romans whose homeland with its fruits and fields and sunshine made life easy, the Saxons were by nature grim and dour. The fight against the dark, gloomy forests and sinking marshlands of their North European homes had left them little time for leisure, and even in the new land to which they had been driven there could be no relaxation, for life became an even more bitter struggle in which not a moment could be left unguarded.

The first arrivals had either to fight or to come to terms with the native Britons who clung, not unnaturally, to the best lands, and the conflict was hard and cruel. Then, once having gained a foothold, the Saxons in possession would turn to fight off the next wave of invaders who also coveted the most fertile areas. Those of the defeated who remained alive, whether defenders or attackers, would be forced to slink into the dense uncultivated forests for their portion of the booty.

Then, after many generations, when the main struggle for land had ended and tiny settlements had been really established, there were constant wars between village and village, tribe and tribe, kingdom and kingdom, which prevented any ease. Even when strong kings gained control, and brought much of the warfare to an end, there was still the unconquered enemy of Nature to be dealt with.

After the great forest clearings had been made with the crudest of tools, the land ploughed with the clumsy ox-plough, the corn sown, and the crops harvested handful by handful with a rough sickle, there was little time or energy for much in the way of pleasure, except food and sleep. And even these simple delights could be enjoyed only in the most favourable of years, for Nature had always a host of reserves to throw into the battle in the shape of a wet summer, a drought, or a cattle plague, any one of which might mean hardship or death to a whole village. Wolves, bears, and wild boars roamed the forests, making life more difficult, and even if man was at peace, and Nature in one of her kindest moods, there were still the savage, cruel, bloodthirsty heathen gods lurking in every dark shadow of the woods to cast a gloom over everything.

It is little wonder, then, that in the early years of their settlement in Britain the Saxons had little time for enjoying themselves, quite apart from their naturally serious character. When one considers the rough hard lives that most of them lived it is not surprising that when they did relax their recreations were often coarse, brutal, and cruel.

As well as being hard, a Saxon's life was precarious: there were few reserves to tide over a lean time, and a poor crop or the loss of a beast might mean the difference between life and death. Tools and equipment were of the simplest so that the yield of the earth had to be torn from the soil by the labour of every member of the family—man, woman, and child. If anyone failed in his duty the whole tiny community might perish; mouths could not be fed unless they provided hands to help with the tilling of the soil and the production of the food. So, at the age of three or four, when children of most ages begin to enjoy the delights of play, the young Saxon was taking a full part in the life and work of his family, keeping starvation at bay.

The very smallest would probably do tasks in and round the hut—preparing food, gathering wood for the fire—while those a little older might be sent to the woods to watch over the pigs scavenging, or to scare birds from the growing wheat. Now, while playing 'houses' or 'farmers' has always been a favourite game with smaller children, it loses much of its fun if they are forced to do it all day and every day.

It seems likely that the average peasant child of the Dark Ages had no manufactured toys at all: the few hours he spent away from the daily tasks would be given to games that prepared him for his grown-up life. He would run, wrestle, fight with sticks, throw stones, and practise with miniature bows and arrows or spears, for all of these were essential in the hard and dangerous struggle to come. For girls there may have been games of make-believe; but the constant round of spinning, weaving, and food preparation can have left little time for recreation at all. Perhaps, as for their parents, the only light in the grey monotonous drudgery was feasting and drinking and warmth. These are the pleasures of beasts—a full stomach, rest from labour, and a warm fire, and the life of poorer Saxon children can have been little better than an animal's, at least in the early years of the period.

But while those in the turf-covered hovel struggled round the year knowing little but work, sleep, and eating, and often barely enough of the last, the nobles in their wooden halls, released from labour in the fields by their slaves and servants, had time to spare. A young nobleman's early life would be a long period of happy training—Running, Wrestling, Cudgel-fighting, Sword-play, Swimming, and Hunting—all preparing him for the first joyous participation in the greatest sport of all: Battle. To the Saxon there was no recreation which could compare. The exhilarating thrill of wielding sword, axe, and dagger in mortal combat was the supreme enjoyment: to win, to plunder the slain, and to bask in the praises of one's followers was pure ecstasy. Even to die in the battle, while naturally not as pleasant as conquering, was not to be despised, for the souls of those killed in battle, it was believed, went straight to Valhalla. There, in Odin's hall, they could fight for evermore, and, being immortal, never suffer death again. The roar and clash of steel on steel could reverberate for ever as unwearying shadows hacked and slashed in eternal combat, which ceased only for orgies of eating and drinking. War, then, was life's greatest gift and pleasure, but when the light faded, and the clangor of sword on shield had been stilled for the day, for those left alive there was the second of the great pleasures—feasting.

Outside the hall the night, the wild beasts, and the dark spirits might rage, but inside the flickering flame-light and choking woodsmoke

Minstrels in a nobleman's hall

wreathed round the rough tables where the battle-weary warriors gorged themselves with abandon. The roasted and stewed hogs, deer, birds, and fish were hacked or torn apart, and washed down with never-ending buckets of ale or mead, or occasionally of imported wine. To stuff with the greed of a pig was a pleasure inferior only to the glory of battle.

Only when they had reached the point when they could take not another morsel would the warriors, drunken to easy mirth or equally easy anger, lurch from the tables to the fire trench. Any other joys in life were minor ones, but even so they were not to be despised, and among the lesser delights the minstrels and gleemen ranked high.

Although he appears in many books, the minstrel who wandered from hall to hall singing, like Tommy Tucker, for his supper, was probably a rarity. The few tracks were so bad, and each settlement so suspicious of strangers, that the life of such a traveller would have been short. The more important halls would probably have professional musicians with a stock of the regular songs and stories, but even in the home of the king himself, as in the more humble dwellings, each man was capable of adding something to the evening's entertainment. Some sang, others recited, some asked riddles, others danced. Indeed, it was a great disgrace to be unable to oblige the company when called upon at table to perform.

In a wealthy noble's home the crude twanging harp of the lowlier hut might be expanded into a small orchestra with several types of horn, straight and curved, flutes, small kettle-drums, and sets of handbells. But this would not be usual, while the harp in one of its forms was found everywhere.

Full, drunk, noisy, red-faced under the grime, and still clutching their ale mugs or horns, the Saxon menfolk would lurch from the table to the fire to sprawl in the straw or to sit on benches near the blaze. The most skilled musician would take up the harp, tune it, and strum his tune, droning one of the traditional ballads he had learned from his father. In a hall of some importance he might improvise some verses flattering his master—an incident that had occurred in the hunt or in battle that day, exaggerated in the hope of reward. Normally, however, the song was one of the well-known epics of the early warriors and their wars, of the heroes who fought with giants and monsters, or of the gods themselves. The harp might be passed from hand to hand, or if no one else was skilled the words passed from mouth to mouth, sometimes each man adding a few lines made up on the instant. Then when the musician was tired or thirsty the men would recite the old tales, which even to-day, translated from the rather rough original, have a beauty all their own.

Riddles were a favourite indoor pastime of the Saxons, and judged by the heavy nature of those which have survived, they were not for the

Juggling to music

more drunken evenings. Probably like the songs and poems, they were handed down from generation to generation with slight variations, and though every one knew the answers, a show of guessing and of giving wrong replies caused much merriment. "There came to a place where many wise men were sitting, a creature with one eye, two ears, two feet, twelve hundred heads, a back, a stomach, two arms and shoulders, one neck and two sides. What was it?" asks one riddle. This impossible creature seems to have been a one-eyed onion-seller, which is rather cheating.

"I am loved by all men, I am found everywhere, and was brought from the woods and valleys and downs. Wings bore me skyward, and carried me to my home under a roof. Then men bathed me in a tub. Now I bind and whip them. I can hurl a young man to the ground. He who fights with me and battles against my strength must crash to the earth if he does not stop in time. I rob him of his strength, his speech, and his might so that he cannot control his mind, his feet, or his hands.

Board-game men

What am I that can bind strong youths, so eager for battle?" asks another The answer is mead, the very strong drink made from the honey of wild bees.

Some riddles seem ridiculously easy, others impossibly hard, but, then as now, perhaps half the fun was in seeing how appropriately the wrong answers given fitted the facts.

The few that have survived were those thought worthy of the precious skill of writing. No doubt the general run of riddles was a much coarser verse, fitted to the rough times, but now much better forgotten.

When the company wearied of the songs, or perhaps when their throats were hoarse with singing, the gleemen gave their entertainment.

A game of hnefatafl on board ship

These, and the gleemaidens who were occasionally seen, were a mixture of acrobat, dancer, and juggler, with a dash of the strong-man and conjuror. In the humblest hall there was usually one villager who could keep the company entertained for a while with leaping, agility, or lightness of foot, but in the more important dwelling there was a troop of professionals who tumbled, jumped, or otherwise performed, often to music.

The dancing does not seem to have been particularly graceful, often consisting of a hopping step, or a curious stamping with knees fully bent to the accompaniment of clapping. Perhaps the most popular of all was the trick of dancing on the hands, with the body upside down, and the legs waving in the air. To this the somersaults, vaults, and general contortions were but a short step and, with occasional feats of strength and skill with weapons, helped to pass the smoky, firelit evenings until the lord and his companions, one by one, fell asleep in the straw.

Although the Saxons took less notice of bad weather than we do to-day, there must have been times when even they were forced to stay indoors. As civilization began to creep from its hiding-place again with the passing of the centuries, there must have been those too who felt that the rowdy eating, drinking, and singing lost some of their novelty after many years. There were always the swords to be sharpened, of course, which could be a pleasant pastime, helmets to be decorated and engraved, and all the other preparations for war made, but when the stronger kings caused much of the local fighting to cease time must have hung heavily on the warrior's hands.

If the real thing was forbidden, or the Saxon was unable to get out to the fields and woods to hunt or to fight, then board games formed a poor but passable substitute, with heavy betting adding a tiny sparkle of excitement. There were certainly two, and possibly three, such games known to the Saxons, and these, together with dice, perhaps replaced much of the rougher entertainment of the early days as the grey light dawned after the Dark Ages.

Dice were used simply as a means of gambling: decorated horns and cups, daggers, brooches, and clasps no doubt changed hands on the fall of the rough bone cubes, and we are told that in their homeland the Saxons would even wager their own bodies, giving themselves as slaves to the winner of the game. Rather more interesting are the dice found in sets of three on a metal rod which may indicate a game on the lines of the Roman *Duodecim Scripta*, which sometimes employed a similar device.

Although no board of this type has yet been found, there are plenty of 'men' which could have been used, and burial mounds are constantly yielding counters of glass, clay, bone, and even amber. The commonest type is a horse's tooth ground roughly into hemisphere, but at the other

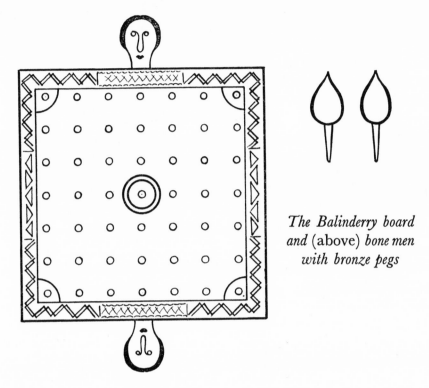

The Balinderry board and (above) bone men with bronze pegs

end of the scale there are the elaborately carved bone 'men' which must once have graced a wealthy nobleman's table.

Although we are not sure whether Backgammon was played by our Saxon ancestors, there is no doubt about the game with the formidable name of Hnefatafl. This was played on a board rather similar to our chessboard with an odd number of squares (thirteen by thirteen, for example), or on a plain piece of wood with rows of holes in it—a very famous board found in Ireland has seven rows with seven holes in each row. The counters—or pegs, in the case of the board with holes—were of two colours, one set white and the other red or black. One player had twenty-four identical men and the other twelve with one extra larger piece. The 'king' was placed on the centre square, or in the centre hole, and was surrounded by his twelve defenders, while the opponent placed his twenty-four 'soldiers' in a definite pattern round the edge of the board.   The king then tried to move, one square, or hole, at a time to the edge, protected by his twelve followers. The hunters tried to capture him by getting one on each side of the king, when he was considered caught, and the game ended. The king's men also could be removed if sandwiched between two of the enemy, but the hunters could not be captured.

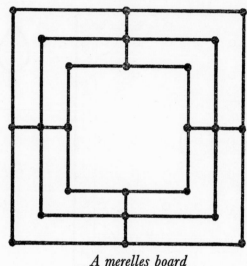

A merelles board

Like the game of Draughts to-day, Hnefatafl could be played idly without using much mental effort, or, if taken seriously, could demand considerable skill, and it is interesting to note that the Saxons thought of a portable board game over a thousand years before the modern pocket chess-sets.

The famous Irish hnefatafl-board had two carved handles, each of which was held by a player who moved his pegs with the other hand. While this seems rather unnecessary on land, where a flat board on a table would be much more satisfactory, if we remember that the Saxons and Vikings were great seamen, the handles make more sense. Anchored for the night, or speeding along under sail, the rowers seated side by side on the lurching oar-bench could hold the board steadily between them, and so pass the weary hours.

A much simpler game was Merelles, a board for which was sometimes found on the back of a flat 'tafl'-board. Three concentric squares were drawn, and the mid-points of their sides joined as shown in the diagram.

A boar hunt

Each junction of lines was a 'point,' twenty-four in all. Each of the two players had five counters which were played one at a time on the points, one black, one white, in an effort to get three men in a straight line, rather like our Noughts and Crosses. If when all five counters had been played neither side had scored, play continued by sliding the men one 'point' at a time, until one player made his row. Then either the game began again, as in Noughts and Crosses, or the successful player was allowed to remove one of his opponent's men.

But though we are told that one king at least played far into the night with his court, indoor amusements were only second-best to the Saxon, whose whole being longed for action. As civilization pushed its tentacles through the forests to put an end to local wars, the wealthy at least found an outlet in Hunting. No doubt many of the poorer peasants who could ill spare the time from their fields also invented excuses to hurry to the woods with spear and bow, for Hunting then could offer much more exciting sport than it could a few centuries later. Wolves, bears, and— best of all—the savage wild boars, roamed freely through the great forests as well as the more familiar deer and small game.

For the noble, either mounted or on foot, the chase was sheer amusement: for the poorer man it was perhaps almost a necessity. But needful or not, there was the same thrill of excitement as the savage, infuriated boar at bay hurled himself at his pursuers, only to be impaled on the barbed boar-spear to the baying of the fierce and powerful dogs. In addition to the delight of the actual hunt and kill, for the peasant at least there was the mouth-watering anticipation of the night's feast, which instead of the everyday porridge of grain would be of flesh such as the earl himself might enjoy.

In the eighth century Hawking seems to have become fairly popular, but this must have been a sport for those with leisure and wealth alone. In the first place, hawks were extremely expensive, and secondly, their training and care called for some skill and a great deal of time, which the peasant could not spare. The poor man too hunted for profit as well as sport, and if a day spent away from the fields resulted in only a couple of cranes or pheasants, instead of the boar which his spear might have earned, there would be empty stomachs to say nothing of the sharp comments of his wife.

Popular though Hunting and Hawking were—and Harold appears on the Bayeux Tapestry with hounds and hawk—they were probably of a rough-and-ready kind, and a full description of these pastimes will be left to the chapter on the Middle Ages when these sports reached their zenith.

If for the majority of the Saxons recreation was savage and crude, their way of life and crowded hours were largely responsible, for given the opportunity they showed that they too could appreciate real beauty. Wealthy women and men delighted in the pleasure of jewellery, their brooches and hair and belt ornaments of gold or silver, inlaid or enamelled with brilliant colours, giving far more joy in the drab years of the Dark Ages than they would to-day in our world of colour.

The Saxon monks too, whose beautiful script was famous throughout Europe, were masters in the art of illuminating manuscripts, and while their painstaking labour could hardly be called recreation, they must have obtained a great deal of satisfaction from glorious vellum pages. The nobles for whom these gospels and psalters were often intended must have enjoyed the splendour, the glowing colour, and the intricate patterns wreathed round the capital letters, and even though few people could read they could pore over the drawings that scrambled up and down the margins of the pages and along the chapter titles.

But these joys were for the very few, and centuries were to pass before the ordinary people shared in the very simplest of them. Progress seemed at a standstill, yet each generation contributed its little towards the general good—an improvement in a plough here, a fatter breed of pigs there, a better cooking-pot somewhere else all saved precious moments of labour, for time is the most important factor in all pleasure. Man, unlike the animal, seeks something other than sleep when he is not working, and when his brain has invented means of easing his toil it will soon turn to creating ways of filling those leisure hours.

D

CHAPTER III

The Middle Ages

AFTER the battle of Hastings, Angles, Saxons, Danes, and Normans seethed and bubbled in the melting-pot until a century and a half later the young English nation emerged. The new race had a character of its own, but bore the imprint of the peoples who had formed it. There was a new nobility, made up largely of Norman families, whose ideas of amusement were a little less bloodthirsty than those of the Saxon nobles; there were many peasants, who, though hard-working, did know their hours of labour, and had at least some time for leisure.

As the three hundred years generally known as the Middle Ages creaked onward a new class of people—town-dwellers—grew up, and their outlook on most things, entertainment included, was different from that of both the countryman and the noble.

Among the aristocracy war was still an interesting pastime, but was no longer the be-all and end-all of leisure. The Crusades, the Hundred Years' War, and the Wars of the Roses gave an opportunity for the wealthy man whose interests lay in military sports to enjoy himself, but many noblemen preferred the thrill without much of the danger and discomfort attached to fighting in the field. Mainly because of this, but partly because King Richard I thought the French knights better than our own in battle, the tournament, which was for many the highest form of entertainment imaginable, was introduced to England. The King may have had other ideas in his mind too, for he charged entrance fees ranging from two marks for a simple knight to twenty for an earl—payable to himself in advance.

The early form of tournament was really a mock battle between two miniature armies at one of the five royal tourney fields—Salisbury, Kenilworth, Wallingford, Brackley, and Blye. For weeks before the event the news was discussed in every castle, manor, and cottage in the district. Carpenters built grandstands and fences on the actual field; armourers and smiths worked hard on armour and weapons; farriers busied themselves with the horses; and the castle cooks laid in vast stocks of food and drink for the revels which preceded and followed the actual fight.

Two days before the contest the leading baron of each of the two sides in the contest set up his pavilion, probably a tent decorated with flags and banners, on the edge of the field. Only gentlemen of the rank of knight or above were allowed to take part, and those who wished hurried to the rival tents to enrol on the side which took their fancy. No doubt the governor of the games saw that the sides were reasonably equally matched in numbers and quality. In the evening all the knights assembled at their respective tents to put their helmets and coats of arms on view on a counter which ran round the pavilion. After the ladies and those not engaged had inspected the strength of the rival teams, every one dispersed for a late night of feasting and dancing.

The following day was occupied in fixing the prizes, and at ten o'clock on the morning of the tournament the governor of the games and his marshals examined all weapons to make sure there was no cheating. If any sword was found to be too sharp it was replaced by a blunted one. The ladies, chattering loudly of their favourites, took their places in the grandstand with those men too old, too feeble, or too cowardly to take part; the clerks who recorded the names of those unhorsed in the battle sharpened their quills at the tables on the edge of the field; and the heralds appointed by the two sides to act as referees took up their positions. The squires fussed over their lords' armour and trappings, tightening here and loosening there.

The two little armies were drawn up behind rope barriers, where they waited, with anxious glances towards the ladies' stand, for the signal for battle to begin. Each man checked his weapons—a blunt sword, and a club by his side—and then the trumpet brayed. The rope dropped, and the horses lurched forward. It is doubtful if there was the spectacular gallop we see in some historical films, for with several hundred pounds of man and iron on its back no horse was capable of great speed.

Each knight picked out his first opponent, and went into the attack while his squire hovered anxiously in the background to pick up a fallen weapon or to adjust armour for his master. The battle surged back and forward, clashing, ringing, and shouting, with an occasional knight retiring from the mass to remove his helmet because of heat. While so defenceless he could not be attacked, but had to replace his armour immediately when so ordered by the governor. The clerks jotted down the names of those unhorsed; the heralds mentally noted points for and against the various knights, and frequently a suspiciously still figure in armour would be dragged from under the thundering hooves. It was undoubtedly very dangerous, for a fall from horseback when encased in iron usually meant injury, if not death under the feet of the horses.

At length a halt was called, and the stiff, bruised, and bleeding contestants hurried home to patch up their wounds and bumps in order to be ready for the evening's merriment, though some of them must have been very heavy dancing-partners after their exploits of the day.

When supper had ended the heralds produced their lists of those whom they thought had fought best, for the prizes were for individual performances, not for the team which won, and handed them to the ladies who made the final decision.

Sometimes as a change from the mêlée a small group of knights would defend a fenced-in area against all comers. This passage of arms was, of course, an imitation of the defence of a castle just as the tournament proper was a mock battle.

The joust in which only two knights took part was considered inferior as a sport to the tourney proper, but, having the advantage that it needed a much smaller ground, it could be played almost anywhere. The competitors were armed with a blunt lance and shield, and charged from opposite ends of the field, the object being either to unhorse one's opponent or to hit him in a vulnerable place. Three points were given for unhorsing, two for a blow on the helmet, one for a hit on the body, while breaking one's lance on the opponent's saddle lost a point. After a number of runs the points were totalled and the winner declared.

At first the joust took place on a strip of open ground, but by the fifteenth century a wooden or rope fence was erected down the centre of the course to prevent the horses colliding, and, perhaps more important, to stop the very real danger of serious injury to an unhorsed knight from the hooves. The horses too were protected by the fence, and, needing less armour for themselves, were able to run more quickly, which made the contest more spectacular.

Perhaps for many the greatest attraction of the tournament was the colour, the pageantry, and the social life, and, after the invention of

The joust

gunpowder, which made the heavily armoured horseman out of date, it was this side of the entertainment which became most important. The skills of horsemanship and weapon-handling almost disappeared in the swirl of the dance and merrymaking.

But at best the tournament probably corresponded to the present fortnight's holiday at the seaside—a treat to be enjoyed or endured once a year. For the remaining fifty weeks the entertainment which surpassed all others, at least for the menfolk, was Hunting. Vast sums were spent by all noblemen in maintaining servants, dogs, and horses for the chase, and so jealously was the game guarded that under the early Norman kings death was the punishment for poaching the king's deer.

The medieval folk seem to have enjoyed Hunting for its own sake— for the skill in tracking, chasing, and outwitting wily animals, and not for the exercise and country air which are largely its attractions to-day. They had, too, a wider range of animals to hunt, for in addition to the deer, which was the accepted king of the forest, there were wild boars and a few wolves as well as wildcats, otters, hares, rabbits, badgers, and foxes, though these last were not considered very good sport.

A wealthy noble to whom the king had granted the right to hunt in certain forests would keep a huge staff of servants under the chief forester to look after the game and chase. There would be foresters, huntsmen, beaters, and especially kennelmen and dogkeepers, whose charges often had more attention and care than the humans themselves. There were greyhounds, both smoothcoated and rough, whose job was to chase the fast deer and hare by sight; the limmers, or hunting-dogs, who were not so fast but followed a trail by scent; the spaniel dogs who chased out birds for Shooting or Hawking, and the huge hounds, rather like Great Danes or mastiffs, whose duty it was to attack savage game, such as boars or wolves, when they turned at bay.

The hunt usually began very early in the morning when the prey was heavy from sleep or overnight-feeding. This put the hunters with their fairly slow horses and dogs on a more even footing. The animals to be pursued were usually located at dawn by the forester, and a hunts-man led the main hunting-party to them to begin the chase. The course might go on all day, the horseman and the followers on foot straggling over large areas of forest and thicket, but a complicated code of signals on the horn let every one know the progress of the hunt.

When at last the kill was made every one stood round the carcass, the hunters with horns blowing *la morte*, those without shouting and hallooing at the tops of their voices, and the dogs, which during the chase had been silent, baying and barking in the general rejoicing before they were given their traditional portion—the neck of the dead animal.

Sometimes when the hunting involved the royal family, high churchmen, or ladies, for all of whom a scramble through the forest might be undignified or dangerous, a different method of killing was used. The forest was fenced off into broad lanes by rope netting on poles, and on the edge of the track a grandstand for the 'hunters' was often built. The foresters were in the woods very early on the morning of the hunt, rounding up the game at one end of the netted run, signalling to the hunting-party by horn blasts the kind, sex, and size of the beasts that were to be expected. When by another burst of horn-code the gamekeeper learned that the party in the grandstand was ready with the correct arrows for the beasts the unfortunate animals were driven past to be shot at by the 'sportsmen.'

When the corpses were collected those not slain by royal arrows were divided up in a traditional method—certain parts for the huntsman, others for the master of game, and others for the foresters.

This seems rather a cowardly method, and for those who preferred to hunt either alone or in small groups, pitting their skill and cunning against the animal's, there was the stalking-horse. This was a canvas horse or deer or ox behind which a hunter with his bow at the ready crouched, gradually wriggling nearer and nearer to his prey. At other times the stalker clothed himself with foliage to approach the unsuspecting prey, rather like a commando during the Second World War.

Although the most noble game was the deer, and the most sporting, according to one writer, the hare, there is no doubt that the most dangerous was the boar. This was hunted on foot, usually with spears to which a crosspiece had been tied just below the head to prevent the boar rushing down the shaft when impaled to attack the hunter. This savage and powerful animal was easily the most terrifying a hunter was called on to face, and the slashing tusks killed many who were unskilled or overconfident. By the Middle Ages, however, it was becoming rare, and was soon, like the wolf, to become extinct in England, so that the nobles were forced to turn to lesser quarries.

Hunting normally involved a great deal of preparation, expense, and ceremonial, but Falconry, or Hawking as it is sometimes called, which was without a doubt the most popular outdoor amusement with ladies, was a quiet, informal pastime in which two or three could indulge at any time, except when the hawks were moulting. It afforded opportunity for exercise, either on horseback or more usually on foot, for conversation or gambling, but it was almost exclusively a sport for the wealthy.

A hawk was a very expensive bird, needed much training, was expensive to feed as its diet included a great deal of poultry, and during the mewing, or moulting-time, demanded highly skilled attention. None of these could the hard-working peasant provide. In addition, the poor man wanted as large a return as possible for his sport in the shape of something fat for the pot, and could not afford to waste time catching a few small birds when the same time spent poaching might result in a hare or deer.

There were two methods of hunting with hawks. In the first, the bird, with the leather hood covering its head and with bells of different tones attached to its legs to tinkle as it flew, was carried on the gloved hand of its master until the prey—usually a heron or duck by the riverside which was a favourite hunting-place—flew up some distance away. The hawk was then unhooded, and flew round in great circles, climbing up and up into the skies until it appeared a tiny dot against the slightly larger dot of its victim. Then it dropped like a stone, or 'stooped,' in hawking language, and with luck two fluttering birds came to the earth, one alive and the other dead. If the mere sport of catching was thought too mild two or more persons could each release hawks and bet on them.

This method was fairly straightforward, and was the one usually adopted by ladies, for the second demanded a much more highly trained bird. The hunter released his hawk when he set out, and it remained hovering at a great height over its master's head as he moved forward with his dogs to rouse the game. As the partridges or pheasants were flushed by the spaniels the hawk dived in to the kill, and then resumed his lofty position in the skies.

Although most of a nobleman's leisure time was spent in the fields and woods with his hounds or hawks, there must have been days when either from inclination or by reason of weather he did not stir far from home. On such days he must often have played Tennis, which had been newly introduced from France, and the only ball game of the many developing in the Middle Ages considered suitable for 'gentlemen.'

The court, often an indoor one, was rectangular, the longer side being

A tennis court

a little over a hundred feet long, and was always bounded by high walls. Running along the two short sides and one long one, and jutting out from the main walls, was a gallery or penthouse which served as a grandstand and also as one of the hazards. On the other long wall, the plain one, a small buttress was built sticking out on the court, to form an additional trap for the ball, and thus to make the game more complicated.

Across the middle of the court, from plain wall to the gallery, a rope was stretched about five feet from the ground to separate the players and to form the major obstacle.

The players, dressed in special clothes and wearing felt slippers for lightness, were armed with racquets which bear a faint resemblance to our modern ones, but were, of course, much more clumsy. The balls of white leather stuffed with dogs' hair must have been much heavier than a modern lawn-tennis ball, and when the game was played, as it sometimes was, with the bare fist instead of a racquet, the knuckles must have become very sore.

Apart from the facts that the ball was hit to and fro across the rope by the racquet or fist and that scoring was 15, 30, 45, advantage, equality, and victory, there is little resemblance to the modern lawn game. A lifetime was needed, it was said, to learn all the complicated rules and skills, for the galleries, the buttress, and other holes and tunnels in various parts of the penthouse led to difficulties at every turn.

Difficult though Tennis was, it was immensely popular with the upper classes who had plenty of free time to master its complications, and plenty of money to provide the equipment. Very different was the lot of the peasant tied to the soil: his only leisure times were the hours on Sunday after church service and on the festivals and holy days of the saints. In these precious hours when work could cease he snatched the simple delights he knew, and high on the list of these were the ball games which needed little equipment or skill.

Handball very similar to the Roman game continued to be played with the same type of leather-covered, bladder-inflated ball, and very often the players wore a hollow wooden brace over their arms and hands to give more power to the blow. From the hand, it was but a short step to the feet, and among the rougher and more vigorous youths Football, or Camp-ball, as it was called, was perhaps the most popular game. The ball for this was similar to the one for Handball except that as the game was much rougher it was stuffed, not inflated. In the case of the more outlandish villages, an animal bladder stuffed with dried peas served the purpose. There seem to have been no rules either of play or about the number of players, whole villages often joining to do battle with neighbouring ones, with the goals perhaps miles apart. Because of the terrible injuries done to players and innocent passers-by who became involved in the tussle, Football was condemned by every serious-minded citizen, by the Church, and was even declared illegal by Parliament. But nothing could stop its progress, and even to-day, in the few places where this medieval game still survives on Shrove Tuesday, shopkeepers barricade their doors and windows.

Goff, or Bandy-ball, the ancestor of our modern Hockey, was a simple game played with small, hard, leather balls stuffed with feathers and a curved club the end of which was shod with a piece of horn or metal. For those who could not afford the proper equipment a simple stick with a knob on the end—a young hazel broken out from the roots is admirable —and a ball turned from the gnarl of a tree were used. The object was to drive the ball between two small sticks set up in the ground or perhaps from one post to another some distance away.

Club-ball, frequently mentioned in old books, seems to have been very similar to our Rounders, the batsman holding a club in one hand, the thrower standing some distance away, and a number of players standing in a circle round the batsman, obviously waiting for a catch. Whether the batsman ran in a straight line or round a circle, or even if he ran at all, is not known, but some form of scoring in this manner seems likely.

Stoolball, a game particularly popular with girls and women, but sometimes played by boys, had very simple origins. The three-legged milking-stool was set up when work was done, and stones were thrown at it. Perhaps because of punishment for damaging the seat, milkmaids soon substituted balls for stones, with one of their number to defend the stool with her fist, hitting the ball aside when she could. Later still a club was used to hit the ball, each hit counting as a point for the defender. From these last two games, Stoolball and Club-ball, our modern game of cricket probably evolved, the wicket from the stool, the running from Club-ball, and the bowler and fielders from both.

One of the most popular of the medieval ball games which has no descendant to-day was Trapball, with its variation, Tipcat, or just plain Cat. For Trapball the ball rested in a hollow at one end of a short seesaw

apparatus, weighing it down. The batsman hit the other end sharply
with his club or bat, and sending the ball into the air, tried to hit it as
far as he could as it came down. What followed depended on the local
rules, because as few people moved about the country, the regulations
for every game varied from place to place. In some games each hit
counted as a point while in others the batsman had to estimate how many
paces he had hit the ball, gaining points for a correct guess, and losing

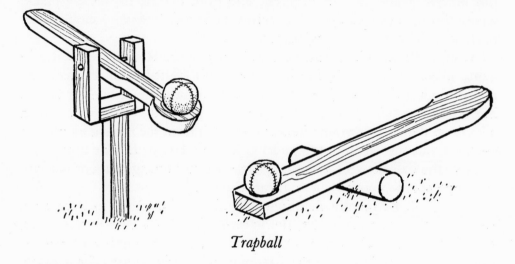

Trapball

them for a wrong one. If the ball was caught by one of the fielders the
bat changed hands.

Tipcat, a similar game, was played with a short length of wood
sharpened to a point at both ends or with a leg-bone of an animal half
in and half out of a hole in the ground. In both cases the 'cat' was
tapped into the air by a sharp blow on the end, and then hit as far as
possible. This game was still being played in 1945, but the trail of
gouged-out eyes, bruises, and spilt blood it left behind, has no doubt led
to its disappearance to-day.

As the countryman grew too old or dignified for the more vigorous
ball games he moved to Quoits, Bowls, Skittles, or Kayles. All these have
much in common, and, with the exception of Kayles, are still played in
one form or another all over the world to-day.

For Quoits an iron spike was driven into the ground with about three
inches protruding, and the players, armed with three or more metal
plates about the size of saucers, stood twenty yards away, and threw

them towards the mark, each trying to get nearest. For those who could not afford the proper metal discs, discarded horse- or ox-shoes made a good substitute, and in this form the game later became very well known in the United States.

There were several variations of the game of Bowls, some being apparently identical with the modern sport, with a small jack and large balls, and with the players, in one fourteenth-century drawing, making those same mysterious handwaving signals that can be seen on any summer evening on the local bowling-green. In other forms of the game the ball had to be driven through arches towards a post, rather like Croquet played on hands and knees.

Kayles was a primitive form of skittles in which a number of conical pins were set up in a straight line about five yards from the players who tried to knock them down by throwing a stick at them. An even cruder form was played by some country folk in which the pins were oxen's leg-bones and the club another.

Skittles seems to have been almost identical with the modern game, and skittle-alleys sprang up all over the country, particularly in the suburbs of towns. One peculiar variation was found in the North of England in which twelve skittles were used in the form of a ring. The missile was a wooden ball cut in half so that when bowled along on the edge it curved in one direction. The half-sphere had to travel the length of the alley and circle right round the group of pins before striking any of the skittles for the throw to count. This game must have demanded great skill indeed.

During hard winters ice sports were popular, and during the Middle Ages it is probable that Skating, as distinct from mere sliding, was introduced. With animal bones strapped to the feet, the skater propelled himself across the ice by means of a stick with an iron point which he wielded between his legs. Some of the younger youths, no doubt those who were Football enthusiasts at other seasons, would charge each other across the frozen pond, using their sticks as battering-rams when they came within striking-distance of each other.

The young, or the old, not to miss the all-too-rare winter sports, sat on blocks of ice "as large as a millstone," and were dragged by others across the frozen surface on these rather uncomfortable sledges.

It is often difficult to enjoy that which one is compelled to do, but the medieval peasants did their best to get some fun from Archery. As

bows and arrows were the mainstay of the English army, kings throughout the Middle Ages constantly repeated the command that every
working-man must have a bow and practise with it on feast days and
Sundays. Shooting at moving targets, at stuffed or tethered birds, or
for prizes all helped to make the sport more attractive, but the fact that
Edward III and other kings made laws under which almost all games
were illegal because of the neglect of Archery shows just how the people
felt.

Although the towns were growing in size during the Middle Ages the
inhabitants could, and did, get easily into the countryside to enjoy the
traditional rural sports which were all that most of them knew. Yet as
people came together in larger and larger groups, new forms of amusement
were bound to grow up. So it was that the travelling showman with his
puppets, his animals, freaks, or acrobats, found it more profitable to
spend much of his time in the cities, playing to bigger audiences, though
he no doubt gave his performances in the villages he passed through when
travelling from one centre to the next.

Foremost among these wandering entertainers were those with
performing animals, for the poor creatures asked for no share in the
profits, and were much cheaper to keep than human artistes. Among
these the dancing bear was the most common though horses who stepped
to the sound of pipe and drum and monkeys who walked on a tightrope
or rode on dogs' backs were often seen. Dogs, perhaps the most easily
trained of all creatures, begged, danced, and went through a variety of
tricks, while one old drawing shows that most timid of creatures, the hare,
beating a drum while strutting on its hind-legs. Birds too gave displays
which seem to us almost impossible.

Unlike modern animal trainers who use nothing but kindness and
rewards to teach their charges, the medieval travelling showman no
doubt used a great deal of cruelty, for the age was a rough one, but this
was nothing compared with the savage inhumanity of the blood-sports—
Bull-, Bear-, and Horse-baiting which began to grow in popularity.

Cockfighting, another of the cruel pastimes, had been practised for
centuries, but was considered rather as a boy's or countryman's sport in
the Middle Ages. On Shrove Tuesday, which seems to have been a day
of special savagery, all the schoolboys of London brought their cocks to
school, and the whole morning was given over to the fights. In rural

Wandering players

areas hurling shells or stones at a cock tied to a post with a yard or two of twine was the great sport for men and boys on the same day, but when all the available birds had been brutally killed every one gathered in the bullring—an open place in the centre of the town or village set aside for such amusements—to watch the baiting.

The unfortunate animal, usually a bear or bull, but sometimes even a horse, was tethered to a post and attacked by dogs in relays while heavy betting went on among the spectators as to how long any particular hound would last or which would be killed first. The more torn and bleeding the shattered animal became, and the higher the heap of corpses which the maddened creature hurled aside in an effort to defend itself, the more the crowd was delighted. And not only among the lowest and more depraved part of the population did this butchery find a following, but all classes from the king downward flocked to the disgusting exhibitions.

In the smaller towns and villages any dog to hand would be set on the victim, but in the larger centres the bulldog was the favourite attacker, as its name implies. Although similar animals had been in existence for centuries, the bulldog was developed by breeding so that it was lower on the ground, to prevent the bull getting its horns beneath, and so that its lower jaw protruded beyond its nostrils. This enabled the dog to keep its grip on the bull's flesh without hindering its breathing, increasing its owner's chance of gaining money in bets.

As a change from the ordinary baiting, or perhaps when an extra-ferocious bear had killed so many dogs that no one was willing to try his animal, men took the place of the attackers. A blinded bear would be whipped from a distance by five or six men who often were attacked by the infuriated creature. One can only say that the human beasts deserved whatever mauling they received.

Although for much of their savage baiting they had to rely on travelling companies of bulls and bears, for lighter entertainment most towns of any size possessed their own resident band of minstrels. These were rather like a combination of the modern town silver band and a troupe of jugglers and acrobats who dressed in uniforms and performed at local festivities. But however skilled the home-bred musicians, the town-folk probably thought more highly of the bands of wandering players, for in addition to melody these brought news of the outside world.

Playing lutes, harps, violins, bagpipes, and pipes and drums, with their singers droning romantic songs, ballads of warlike deeds, the lives of saints or far more often coarse, humorous ditties, they would stand in the market-place, dusty and travel-stained, while the crowd gathered. The songs ended, the jugglers would begin tossing knives, balls, and cups into the air; the acrobats would begin their tumbling and leaping while the balancing expert poised upside down on the points of swords or tottered over the cobbles with a pole surmounted by a plate on the top of his nose. Most of the 'modern' tricks could be seen in a medieval street, and perhaps far more, for the people to whom these displays were a novelty could be easily deceived.

A collection would be taken at the end of the performance, but the minstrels could expect little from those who had little themselves, so that after gossiping to the townsfolk of the news, genuine, rumoured, and deliberately untruthful, they would pass to the hall of one of the noblemen to give their performance again there. Much of these wandering show-men's livelihood came from the gifts in kind—food, clothing, and footwear—given to them after these private entertainments, but their purses were always open to any contribution, however acquired.

The minstrels' glory, however, had passed its zenith: it belonged to a land of villages and manor-houses. The growing towns, though still tiny, were striking out on their own, and without a doubt their greatest contribution to the world of entertainment was the theatre. Though this may well have been born in the country as in the city, it was the city which, through the centuries, saw it grow from its simple and humble beginnings to the robust stage proper.

Drama was born in the Church, and quite early in the Middle Ages the parish priests began to act simple scenes from the Bible at the great religious festivals of Easter and Christmas. These were very short episodes played before the altar, perhaps to instruct the people in the more important Scripture stories, perhaps to vary the long services conducted in Latin which few ordinary members of the congregation knew. The plays themselves were at first in Latin, but soon the priests, dressed simply in robes to show the characters they represented, spoke in English.

The medieval folk were delighted with this new form of entertainment, and audiences became so large that the tiny playlets had to be trans-ferred to the steps at the west door of the church while the townsfolk

E

stood in the churchyard. Just as the Roman playgoers were not too sure who was who in their comedies and dramas and had to be helped in their identification by masks and robes, so the medieval peasants were sometimes confused by the mass of actors, especially in the Easter plays. To help them, small raised platforms were placed left and right of the altar or west door, each one representing the positions of one of the characters. In one series of Easter plays the platform immediately on the left of the altar was always the sepulchre and that on the right a prison. The next platform to the left of the tomb, dressed with curtains and foliage so that only the upper part of the persons standing on it was showing, was always Heaven. On the right of 'prison' was a dais representing Hell, where several actors beat kettles and made a loud wailing noise. On the left again were in order Mary, the Disciples, and Nicodemus, while on the right were the stands for Pilate, Caiaphas, and Joseph. Hell was often made in the form of a whale's mouth through which the wicked crept to their punishment.

It was not long before the Church began to wonder if it had done the right thing, and whether the huge congregations were present for religious reasons or for entertainment. But the public, having once acquired a taste for the drama, would not give it up easily, and when the priests were forbidden to give performances outside the church it was fortunate that the trade guilds, then growing strongly in the towns, took over the duties.

The miracle plays, as they were called, were worked up into long, continuous cycles, involving many scenes from both the Old and New Testaments, each episode being performed by one group of craftsmen. Often the scene selected had some bearing on the amateur actors' trades —fishmongers might act the story of Jonah, the carpenters that of Noah building the Ark, and the goldsmiths and silversmiths usually gave the Christmas scene with the Wise Men presenting their traditional gifts.

These plays were performed on what were really movable stages built on wheels high up from the ground. The space below the acting-floor, among the wheels and axles, was curtained round, and used as a dressing-room, while the roof of the vehicle was sometimes used as Heaven, characters being drawn skyward by means of ropes and windlasses. The whole procession would move into one part of the town on the day appointed for the showing, give a full performance, and then move to the next street or square where the show would be repeated.

At first the plays kept strictly to Biblical characters, but gradually

Miracle plays

people and scenes not in the Testament stories began to creep in. The smiths at Coventry, for example, in their play of the trial of Jesus, had, besides God, Peter, Judas, Pilate, Caiaphas, and Malchus, two princes, four tormentors, two knights, Pilate's son, Herod and his wife, a porter, and the devil. Although the Scriptural characters were probably always reverently treated, the invented ones were often comics, and indulged in

A puppet theatre

slapstick humour which made the plays even more popular with the audiences. The chief comic was often the devil, who was later to become the fool in real stage plays.

Towards the end of the Middle Ages the miracle plays began to be replaced by the moralities, which were acted on the same movable stages and by the same tradesmen-actors. These were not true Biblical stories but short dramas in which virtues and vices became real people and walked the platforms. Thus, in the most famous morality of all, *Everyman*, the hero is summoned to go the journey of death, and Wealth, Friends, Good Deeds, Repentance, and Confession, all real people, are involved in his final salvation.

Closely connected with the miracle plays were the puppet theatres, portable booths very much like our modern Punch and Judy show, but rather more attractive. The medieval audience could not hiss and cheer Mr Punch's antics, however, for he had to wait for several centuries more to be invented. It is most probable that the puppet plays were very similar to those of the larger movable stages, based on Bible stories. Perhaps even the moralities may have been performed by the jointed wooden dolls prancing up and down on strings or sticks.

But drama, whether with live or wooden actors, was largely a daylight entertainment in the Middle Ages, and although the draughty, cold, and gloomy medieval homes did not encourage late nights, there must have been a gap between the end of daylight and the beginning of sleep. As few could read, and as books were rare and expensive, to say nothing of the strain on eyesight in peering at the crabbed writing in the flickering tallow lights, some entertainment had to be sought, especially for the winter nights.

In the wealthy home this was easy because there were always the resident minstrels, acrobats, and tumblers if no wandering troupe were in the district. The musicians and storytellers could add their store to the fun, and if everything else failed there was the fool, or jester. Sometimes this character with his coloured dress, horned cap, and wand was a genuine simpleton who in his idiocy could be teased and provoked, and who did not understand his own mad behaviour. At other times the fool was a highly intelligent man whose sparkling wit and quick mind could turn any chance remark to laughter. The jester had great freedom, and could often make remarks to his master for which anyone else would have been savagely punished if not put to death.

But noblemen must have often tired of this noisy junketing and demanded something quieter in their own chambers. The humbler homes too had to be entertained when outdoor amusements could not be had, and so the range of indoor games gradually grew.

Dice were as popular as ever, and gambling and cheating seem to have flourished if we judge by the loaded dice which have been found. Cross and Pile, or, as we call it, Heads or Tails, which is now used mainly to settle issues on which agreement cannot be reached, was immensely popular as a game in its own rights. Edward II is said to have wagered thousands of pounds, tossing coins with his courtiers far into the night.

Moving away from such simple games of chance, we find draughts being played under the name of Ladies' Game, or the Game of Ferses, but it was not particularly popular until the fifteenth century. Some exquisitely carved draughtsmen up to three inches in diameter have been found, however. Chess was also known, but was not very widely played, possibly because of the difficulty of the game.

Although Chess requires concentration, it was a child's sport compared with Rithomomachy, or the Philosopher's Game. For this fantastically complicated game, which was played on a double chess or draughts board, each player had twenty-four pieces, eight triangular, eight circular, and eight square. Each piece was numbered, the whites based on an even series of figures and the blacks on an odd. Thus the whites included as well as the usual 2, 4, 6, such peculiar numbers as 49, 289, 169, 91, 153, and 45, while black ranged from 3, 5, 7, to 190, 225, and 361. One triangle, one square, and one circle of each side were stacked together to form a king, or pyramid, white's pyramid having a total 91 and black's 190.

For moving, circles moved one square, triangles two, and squares three, but the real complication came when a capture was attempted. There were many rules, the two simplest being the multiplication and addition captures. If, for example, white square 15 was three squares from black's 45 (remembering a square could move three places) the black could be removed because $3 \times 15 = 45$. For the addition method imagine white circle 36 was one square from black 45, and white triangle 9 was two places off. Because 9 and 36 make 45 and both pieces are in their correct jumping-distance, the black 'man' could be taken off, and one of the two whites put in its place.

The object of the game was to capture the pyramid or to make it impossible for the piece to be moved, but even when this had been done the game had not ended. The victor had then to 'triumph'—that is, to arrange his men in complicated series of mathematical progressions. It is little wonder the game was played only in the most learned society.

Easily the favourite indoor games at all levels were Merelles, Fox and Geese, and Backgammon, but towards the end of the fifteenth century playing-cards, introduced a century earlier, were beginning to increase in favour.

Merelles, which had been played in Saxon times, was universal from palace to hovel, and the monks seem to have been specially fond of it, for boards are frequently found scratched on cloister floors. The simplest game, Three Men's Morris, was played on Board No. 1, and the object, as in the Saxon game, was to get three men in a row. When this had been done the game started again. On Board No. 2 five counters were used, and on the one illustrated on page 46, nine to twelve, the most usual being Nine Men's Morris. For these games the counters were placed one at a time on the points until three were in a straight line, when the successful player was allowed to remove any one of his opponent's pieces. If, however, when all the men had been put on the board neither side had scored, the pieces were moved in single steps until a decision was reached. Play continued until one player had only two counters left and was thus unable to form a row.

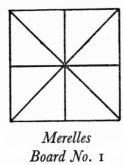

Merelles
Board No. 1

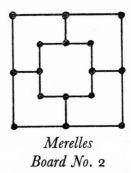

Merelles
Board No. 2

Backgammon, identical with the modern game and known as Tables in the Middle Ages, was the indoor pastime of the solid yeomen, crafts-men, and merchants, particularly as they grew older. Rithomomachy and perhaps Chess were a little too complicated for them, and Merelles and Fox and Geese they probably thought of as games for youths and rustics. If they wanted a staid family pastime, then Backgammon was the game for them; if they craved a little more excitement, then they could gamble on the result, and all the while the element of chance with the fall of the dice was tempered with just enough skill in choosing the moves to make the game interesting.

Fox and Geese, though played everywhere, did not enjoy the standing of Tables, but nevertheless it did demand some skill. The pieces began as shown on the board in the diagram, the fox being in the centre and the geese to one side. All pieces could move one step at a time in any direc-tion, but the fox was permitted to capture the geese by jumping over them as in Draughts. The geese had no powers of taking, and the object of the game was to surround the fox so that he could not move. The fox could win by capturing so many geese that it was impossible to trap him.

In the hands of a skilful player the game was too easy for the geese could always win. To make the sides more equal, two more geese were added in the fifteenth century, and at the same time only the fox was allowed to move diagonally. In this form, and with other variations, the game was played as late as the 1930's, and perhaps still is.

Although in the Middle Ages the same pastimes were played by both young and old, small children revelling in the barbarous baitings and grown-ups prancing round in ring games, there were some amusements

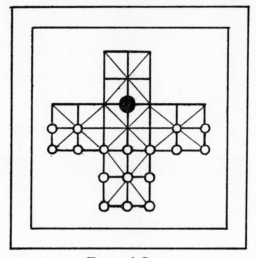

Fox and Geese

which were children's alone. Differences in wealth and social standing always seem much less in childhood, and the amusements of the young lord and the young peasant are much more alike than those of their parents. This was true of the Middle Ages, though the sons of noblemen had a particular round of amusements designed to fit them for their adult life.

Much of a young lord's recreation consisted of training for the adult sports in the hunting-field, the tournament, and the battle proper. He would be a horseman, naturally, riding from a very early age, and practice with weapons, both in and out of the saddle, would fill much of his earlier years. The most effective training pastime, however, and the most amusing—for the spectators—was the quintain.

This was a stout post fixed upright in the ground which the young knight, dressed in armour and carrying his shield, attacked, chopped, hacked, and stabbed with sword. Often weapons of double weight were

The quintain

used to strengthen the muscles. Sometimes a wooden figure rather like a tailor's dummy, and usually representing a Saracen, was used to make the attack more realistic.

Another form of the quintain which was not quite such a defenceless opponent as the fixed one, had a beam pivoted on the top of the post with a square- or shield-shaped target at one end and a leather bag filled with sand or stones hanging from the other. The main object of this kind was probably to teach the horseman to swerve after striking a blow, for if he did not move quickly aside with his horse after hitting the wooden target with his lance, the beam would swing sharply round, and the bag would strike him on the back of the head, often throwing him to the ground.

The less fortunate children could not of course afford horses for this sport, but it caught the imagination of all classes, and poorer boys mounted on horse-headed sticks, on wooden horses on wheels drawn by their friends, on each other's backs and on foot, charged with their wooden poles. But whether one actually performed or not, there must have been a lot of amusement watching others ruefully rubbing their heads after a poor charge.

Sometimes—though this must have been for pure amusement without any thought of military training—the quintain took the form of a pole on the top of which was balanced a barrel of water, the object being to dislodge the tub without getting wet. At other times a target was mounted in the middle of a river, and the attacker stood with his pole on a platform in the bows of a boat rowed by his friends. A false stroke here would send him headlong into the water, much to the delight of the people crowding the banks. As many boys learnt to swim (using bundles of reeds as waterwings in the early stages), it was probably quite amusing for the victim too.

All children would have joined in the ball games, and with Marbles, Shuttlecock, Hopscotch, and Pegtops, there was no shortage of innocent outdoor amusements. Flying kites and running with windmills—the sails fixed to the end of the pole instead of to the side as they are to-day—kept the younger ones amused, but with the shooting of clay pellets, stones, or seeds through a tube in the fashion of a peashooter, a rather more dangerous element began to creep in.

Less likeable were the cruel games played especially by country children, but these sprang from a genuine failure to realize that animals had feelings, and not from sheer delight in inflicting pain. The throwing of clubs at tethered cocks by youths has already been mentioned, and these same boys had most probably served an apprenticeship at Chafer- or Butterfly-spinning. For this very popular and very detestable sport the insect was speared by a pin or hook to which was attached a fine thread. The poor creature was allowed to escape and fly away, then

Windmill   *Pegtop*   *Skates*

drawn back, fluttering by the thread. Fortunately, this wretched amusement, which lasted for many centuries, is now dead.

Indoors Blind Man's Buff and Piggy in the Ring were the favourites if we judge by the drawings that have come down to us, though no doubt there were many more round games. We know the names of many of these—Hand-in-and-hand-out and Penny-pricks are two among many—but we have no idea how they were played.

Toys, as such, seem to have been relatively rare, and the few that have been left on record for us are almost exclusively for boys. Girls in the Middle Ages seem to have been badly catered for altogether in the matter of amusements, apart from dancing. While it is likely that from a very early age most of their time was occupied with helping their mothers with household tasks, it is unlikely that girls managed completely without dolls in one form or another, but none have survived. Perhaps with the large families common in the Middle Ages there was always a live doll needing attention, a task which the hard-pressed mother was only too willing to hand over.

Most of the boys' toys were connected with warfare, and in addition to the wooden hobby-horses, miniature weapons and armour of the more fortunate, there were the model soldiers. There were both metal and wooden infantry men and mounted knights, but more interesting than the purely stationary figures were the moving ones. Some of the foot-soldiers had a small hole in the chest, through which a cord was passed. If the model's feet just touched a solid surface and the cord, usually held across a table-top, was alternately slackened and tightened slightly the figures moved slowly forward or backward. A pair of such soldiers with their strings running parallel close together and worked by two children could be made to fight quite realistically.

The jousting toy was more elaborate, consisting of a knight with lance extended, mounted on the back of a horse on wheels. The warrior was hinged at the saddle so that he would topple backward if tapped smartly on the upper part of his body. Two boys, each pushing or pulling his model forward on a table, would try to get his knight's lance to overthrow his opponent, and thus score a point.

But these and all other toys were unusual: children's amusements in the Middle Ages, even more than adults', depended on 'doing' rather than 'having.' As everything had to be made slowly and painfully by hand, skilled craftsmen could not afford to devote their time to the manufacture of articles whose only use was recreation. Tools and house-hold equipment came first, so that games usually demanded no equip-ment at all—racing, chasing, and fighting—or else the very simplest. Sticks, stones, berries, nuts, flowers, and, unfortunately, living creatures were the main items of sports gear. The games themselves were often coarse, cruel, and dangerous, but in them lay the seeds which in the milder, kinder climate of later centuries were to grow to the pastimes we enjoy to-day.

Medieval toys

CHAPTER IV

Tudor Times

THE Tudor period in the story of games is, as it is in many other aspects of our history, a bridge between the old and the new. At one end the reign of Henry VII is firmly rooted in a medieval war, medieval people, and medieval customs; at the other the death of Queen Elizabeth I stands at the beginning of the modern world. By the time Henry VIII's tempestuous reign had passed and the effect of the Renaissance and religious changes had made themselves felt throughout Europe, the old order was changing: new ideas travelled more freely from land to land, the old chivalry was dying, and, most important of all, there was a new freedom abroad. No longer were there only two main classes, noble and peasant, for the new merchants and traders were a stepping-stone, up or down.

As the sixteenth century rolled on its exciting way, life in England became more and more civilized in the present meaning of the word, and hand in hand with the improvements in building, food, habits, and customs went a moderating influence in pastimes.

Hunting and Hawking were still the great recreations of the nobility although even here a new element began to creep in. Following, out-witting, and killing a wild beast were not now the only objects of the chase, for Hunting, particularly under Elizabeth I, tended to become a formal occasion with magnificent forest picnics to the accompaniment of music. With so many more men becoming involved in business and city life there was a growing need for more exercise too, which the hunt offered. The country gentleman, however, continued to chase, as his medieval forefathers had done, in the woods which rapidly dwindled as farming grew in size and importance.

For the peasant too, who now shared in the country's general pros-perity, there was more chance of a day's sport, for the savage laws against poaching were made much less severe. Elizabeth I, for example, reduced the period of imprisonment for stealing or breaking hawks' eggs from a year and a day to three months, and even then the lighter sentence was probably rarely enforced.

Hunting was beginning to feel the effect, very slight at first, of muskets, and towards the end of Elizabeth's reign the battle between bows and guns was raging in real earnest. For the whole of the Tudor period the clumsy firearms were much less accurate and much more unreliable than bows, particularly the crossbow, but of course some huntsmen may have considered that the likelihood of the early gun to explode and kill or injure the shooter rather than the animal added a certain thrill to the sport.

While a stag or even a boar offered a reasonably sized target to the erratic muzzle-loading firearm, a swiftly moving bird high in the air was impossible for the wandering shot from the ancient musket, so in his field the hawk still reigned supreme. Any duck or heron that was shot was usually asleep or at least caught unawares on the ground. The relaxing of the severe laws and the increased spare time available caused the sport of Hawking to spread to humbler people, and it was a poor yeoman indeed who could not boast of his bird. Books on the training and care of hawks poured from the newly invented press, and no doubt these helped many who might otherwise have hesitated, though in the matter of Falconry reading was a poor substitute for experience.

Besides the names of the actual birds, a whole vocabulary grew up round Hawking, and the conversation of Tudor people discussing their favourite sport would be as incomprehensible to us as 'late cuts,' 'bully offs,' and 'body swerves' would have been to Henry VIII. There were hot disputes over the rival merits of the different training methods to be adopted: was the eyas, a hawk which had been reared by hand from a nestling and was as a result very tame but sometimes lacking in spirit, better than a ramage hawk, which had been captured after it had led a wild life for a few months after leaving the nest? Or perhaps the haggard hawk, a full-grown bird with several seasons of life on its own in the woods before capture, and often untameable, was preferable to either, for if its spirit could be broken its savagery and bravery was unsurpassed. So the debates raged in castle and in cottage.

As in the Middle Ages, the nobleman and his wife flew the merlin or the peregrine falcon, both majestic, long-winged, and expensive, while the countryman made more and more use of the goshawk, sparrow-hawk, and kestrel. These, with their short wings, might not have had the grace of their larger cousins, but their returns for the pot in the shape of rabbits and low-flying birds were fairly certain, and poorer folk had to consider their next meal as well as a few hours' recreation. Their stubby wingspan too made the lowlier hawks more suited to the bushy and wooded countryside which the countryman normally used as his hunting-ground.

Another sport in which all classes of people joined was Coursing. This was merely chasing hares, or rabbits if a hare was not available, with dogs. The wealthy man would use his thoroughbred greyhounds, the peasant and farmer his fastest mongrel, but, whichever was used, a fair start was usually given to the quarry to make the chase more equal. As often as not the animal escaped, but the courser had no hard feelings—he had had excitement and exercise and most probably felt ready for his supper, even though the hare that might have formed it was safe in its form.

The increasing use of cannon and smaller firearms for warfare throughout the sixteenth century made the heavily armoured knight and his lance out of date so that the tournament, whose main task was to improve the knight's skill and give him an opportunity to show his paces, became rather unnecessary, despite the efforts of the Tudor kings. Henry VIII, an immensely strong, athletic man, who delighted in battle because he usually won, tried hard to restore it to its former glory, but failed. The tourney was kept going, mainly for the dancing and social life it offered, though some combats and tests of skill did still take place. These, however, became milder and milder as the years passed; the jousting-yard, for example, was often covered with a deep layer of straw and mulch to soften the blows for those knocked from their horses—much to the disgust of the veterans.

In many tournaments too the joust was replaced by the harmless sport of Tilting at the Ring which, although introduced a century or two earlier, was not bloodthirsty enough for the Middle Ages. For this pastime the knights, wearing little or no armour, galloped swiftly, in complete safety, along the tilt-yard to catch on the point of their lances a small metal ring about an inch in diameter, which was suspended from a post on the side of the track. If speared cleanly and accurately the ring slipped from its clip, and was carried off on the point of the weapon to the end of the course. The winner was the rider who captured the ring the greatest number of times in a certain number of runs. After the joust proper, with real opponents for a mark, this was rather like asking a veteran big-game hunter to spend his time shooting at paper targets with an air pistol.

To satisfy those who still liked a little violence but did not wish to run too great a risk of injury, the 'baston course' was invented in the fifteenth century and became popular in the sixteenth. The two contestants, usually on foot, stood one each side of the wooden fence of the tilt-yard, carrying a heavy club shod with iron, and wearing an exceptionally large helmet thickly padded inside to prevent damage to the head. On top of the helm was the knight's crest—the tail of a fox, a stuffed bird, or some equally fanciful creation—the object being to batter one's opponent's emblem to pieces. Even if the padding deadened the effect of the blows the clang of iron club meeting steel helmet must have been deafening and uncomfortable for the person inside, but at least there was little danger of fatal injury because of the height of the wooden partition.

About the middle of the century the long tuck, or rapier, was introduced to England from the Continent, and immediately the fashion of fencing took hold of those who a century earlier would have been the firmest supporters of the tournament. The craze took the aristocratic circle like a whirlwind though some of the old-fashioned knights spoke bitterly of the new weapon, and yearned for duels with the old English, two-edged broadsword and round shield that they had used in their youth. The flexible, pointed rapiers grew longer and longer until Elizabeth I had to make an order forbidding any to exceed a yard in length. She had responsible men stationed at the gates of towns to break off the tips of any offending weapons so that they were the right length, and her officers carried out their task most ruthlessly and efficiently.

Schools of fencing, often with foreign masters, sprang up all over the larger towns, offering tuition in either the Italian or Spanish methods of fighting. The Italian method was eventually adopted, but at first the Spanish style, with its formal movements almost like a complicated dance based on a geometric pattern, was the more popular. In this the opponents moved round the circumference of a circle of such diameter that their rapier-tips just touched when held out at arms' length, and advanced to the attack by a series of steps, placing their feet only in certain very definite positions. To teach would-be duellists the correct footwork, a large circle with intersecting chords was drawn on the floor

F

of the school. The pupil was allowed to step only where the lines crossed, and thus was supposed to acquire the perfect motions. The arm movements were almost as complex, so that the whole thing became almost a mental exercise and of little use in actual fighting unless one's opponent played fair and obeyed the same intricate rules.

With so many gentlemen trained in fancy swordsmanship and always carrying their rapiers by their sides, it is not surprising that they soon resorted to duelling as a means of settling differences. Although this can hardly be called a sport, it was encouraged by the Queen, and rapidly became at least a minor pastime of a certain section of the upper classes.

Tennis, which had begun in the Middle Ages, grew in popularity throughout the sixteenth century, but the expense of the equipment and court, whether built indoors or in the now disused moat of a castle or manor-house, made the game fashionable only with the upper classes. Humbler folk had neither the money to spend on racquets and balls nor the time to waste acquiring the skills and learning the complicated rules. But though Tennis was not among their favourite recreations, the less wealthy did not lack means of amusing themselves.

By far the greater part of the population of England still lived in the villages, and loved festivals as much as the people of the Middle Ages. The increased wealth of England and the general higher standard of living made it possible for the ordinary man to enjoy more leisure time than the medieval peasant with his dawn-to-dusk toil, but as England at the Reformation lost most of the feast days of the Church, which had been holidays in earlier times, other opportunities for entertainment had to be found. Harvest feasts, Church-ales, weddings, christenings, funerals, and local games such as those held in the Cotswolds, all formed an excuse for the traditional country sports, but without a doubt the favourite was May Day which, though celebrated from early times, now became much more important.

Very early on May 1 all the younger folk from the villages—and towns too, for everywhere was still within easy reach of the countryside—poured into the woods to collect branches of greenery. The maypole, if not already erected, was put up on the village green, and decorated with garlands, flowers, and coloured ribbons to the noise of laughter and teasing. The boughs and twigs left over were often made into bowers to be used later in the day's revels for shade or shelter.

Maying breakfasts were held in the dewy woods when the foliage had

The fencing school

all been gathered, so that as soon as the pole was ready the fun began, usually with the dancing of jigs and other country steps. The ribbon dances we usually associate with maypoles were not part of 'merry England,' and, like Christmas-trees, were introduced to the country during Queen Victoria's reign.

For the rest of the day no work was done, the hours of daylight and long after being given over to eating, drinking, games, dancing, and general jollifications. The younger folk would fight with sword and buckler (the rapier had not yet reached the peasant in his village), cudgels, or quarterstaff, wrestle (particularly in the North and in Cornwall), run races, jump, hurl the sledgehammer, throw the bar (rather like Tossing the Caber in Scotland), and shoot with bows and arrows, for prizes. For those whose bones would no longer stand the violence there were Quoits, Skittles, Kayles, and Loggats—this last game consisting merely of throwing a clublike stick at a small post. A game called Billyards may have belonged to the out-of-door games, perhaps a kind of croquet, for when it later appeared as the indoor game we know— billiards—the green cloth was said to represent the grass.

So the day would pass, with, after the Reformation, the fun of half a dozen of the former saints' days squeezed into one mad whirl of excitement. By evening even the young folk, whose day it really was, were tired. Bonfires might be lit, but on the whole, as the nights were still cold, the older people moved the festivities to tavern and home, and left the May moonlight to the younger people and romance.

Although officially it earned a penalty of up to six days' imprisonment, Football still pursued its noisy, wild, and highly dangerous course across the fields and ditches for most of the year, and quickly spread to the apprentices in the towns, where innocent bystanders in the streets were involved in the brawls. Even wilder was Hurling, in which a wooden or cork ball was carried by hand in a primitive Rugby fashion. All pretence of order disappeared, and the game developed into a free fight as the 'players' battled to get the ball from one goal to the other, often a distance of four miles. The name Hurling was also given to a savage and bloodthirsty ancestor of Hockey, which found its way from Ireland to England, and became popular in some areas. This has led to some confusion, but, though the games were completely different, the trail of broken heads and limbs they left seem to have been remarkably similar.

Club-ball, Bandy-ball, Trapball, Goff, and Stoolball flourished as
country amusements for a more gentle mood, though even these would
cause a modern referee some dismay. Stoolball, as we said in the previous
chapter, was probably similar to Rounders, except that it may have had
milking-stools for the bases, and must have been a specially quiet pastime,
for it seems to have been a custom in Tudor times for young men and
ladies to play for kisses as the prize, especially on May Day. Whether
the teams were mixed or were boys against girls, and whether the losers
or the winners collected the kisses, we are not told.

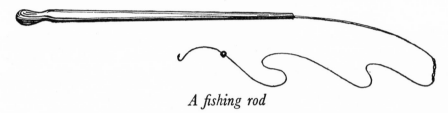

A fishing rod

Even though Hawking and Coursing as pastimes were spreading into
humbler homes, the amusements of the rich and poor were still on the
whole largely separate. One sport, however, from its earliest beginnings,
was a favourite with men of all classes, and women too, if we are to
judge by the fact that the first written instructions in English on the
subject are supposed to be by a lady. In the *Boke of St Albans*, a volume
attributed to Dame Juliana Berners, Prioress of Sopwell in the mid-
fifteenth century, is a section entitled *Fysshynge wyth an Angle* which gives
us a delightful picture of how the angler prepared for, and spent, his
leisure hours by pond or stream four hundred years ago, and if all the
fearsome preparations described by Dame Julia had to be gone through
to-day there would be far fewer intent figures along the banks of canals
and rivers.

As each fisherman had to make his own rod, the question of expense
did not enter into consideration, and we are given exact instructions for
the somewhat tricky operation of manufacturing an 'angle.' A willow-
or hazel-branch, nine feet long, was hollowed out (for lightness) with
red-hot iron rods while bound to a bench with rope to prevent warping.
To the top of this was fitted a yard-long length of hazel, and then the
last four or five feet were of whippy blackthorn, crab, or juniper wood.

The line was tied to the tip of the rod, and consisted of strands of hair
from the tail of a white horse, plaited six thick, and dyed with vegetable

colouring. Dame Julia recommended a green line for the summer months when the water was clear, yellow for the autumn, to match the dying rushes and leaves, and brown for winter when the stream was stained with stirred-up mud. There was, of course, no question of a reel for several centuries after the time of *Fysshynge wyth an Angle*.

Floats of cork, ranging in size from a pea to a walnut, were fastened to the line, and the whole apparatus finished off with a barbed hook made from a needle bound to the line.

For bait, beside the usual worms and grubs, there were many artificial flies made of dyed wool and feathers, and, rather cruelly, of live frogs. *Fysshynge wyth an Angle* tells us that for really good sport you must fasten a short fishing-line baited with a live frog to the foot of a goose. Then when the bird is released on a pond containing pike the struggle between fish and fowl will be a delight to watch. But this was exceptional, and the Tudor angler usually flourished his clumsy rod as patiently and with as much—or as little—success as the present-day fishermen does his graceful one. The only advantage he may have had was that as the waters were not so heavily fished as nowadays there was possibly more to catch.

Although by Tudor times roads had improved a little and communications in general were better, the countryman, who was always suspicious of change, was still largely content to amuse himself as his ancestors had done. It was in the growing towns, therefore, that the most important changes in entertainment took place, and in this connexion it is rather depressing that the Elizabethans, with their love of music, poetry, and beauty generally, should have taken such delight in the bloodthirsty tormenting of animals which gained such prominence in the sixteenth century. It is true that the baiting of bulls and bears and Cockfighting had been popular in the Middle Ages, but on the whole they had been haphazard and unorganized. Among the Tudor people, who ought to have grown out of such pursuits, they became the national sports of the country, at least among the lower and middle classes.

Henry VIII was largely responsible for the growth of Cockfighting, and under his orders the first tiny arena, or cockpit, where these birds fought, was built at St James's in London. Elizabeth I too was a keen follower of this sport, which was particularly popular as a Sunday-afternoon recreation, and as such was much frowned upon by the Puritans. The savage little birds, made more dangerous by being fitted with

A bear pit

razor-sharp steel spurs on their legs, slashed and pecked each other to death for the delight of the screaming spectators, who gambled furiously on the result of the battles.

Sometimes a main, or match, consisted of a series of duels between equally savage birds; at other times a number of cocks were thrown into the ring to fight until one alone was left alive, bleeding and torn. Usually the birds fought to the death, but occasionally one would turn tail and flee, whereupon the whole assembly would jeer both cock and its owner. Noise, in fact, was invariably linked with the cockpit, and writers of the time are never tired of describing the unrestrained fury of shouting and quarrelling which let the outside world know that a contest was in progress.

In Henry VIII's reign, too, the first amphitheatre was built at Southwark for the baiting of bulls and bears. Before this the performances had taken place in the open in market-squares and on village greens, and no doubt still continued to do so, but the erection of a theatre especially for the 'sport' indicates how organized it had become. The hundreds of spectators which the building would hold each paid a penny admission, with another penny for the best places in the gallery where they could watch the cruel sport in comfort.

A second arena near by, the famous Paris Garden, was later built by Elizabeth I, and devoted entirely to the baiting of bulls, while the older building was then used for bears. Herds of both kinds of animal were bred especially for the baiting, and the two arenas had a resident 'staff' of seventy mastiffs on the premises, ready to do battle with any comer.

The names of the more ferocious bears, like those of famous racehorses to-day, became known throughout the country, and poets sang the praises of Harry Hunks, Tom of Lincoln, and Blind Robin. All of these were the victors of scores of contests, but there were thousands of others not so fortunate. It has been said in the Elizabethans' favour that the bears, being such valuable animals, were rarely killed but after a battle were nursed back to health. Perhaps, however, death was better than a lifetime of murderous maulings with a slow and painful stretch of convalescence between.

Like Cockfighting, baiting was largely a Sunday pastime, and perhaps drew the worst elements of the population, particularly in the cities. The Government, however, encouraged the sport, thinking that if the mob was completely absorbed with the betting beforehand, the actual performance, and the discussion and argument afterwards, it would not turn its mind to the more dangerous practice of planning rebellions against a throne which for the first half-century at least was not very secure.

If in the field of entertainment the Tudor folk darkened their record by their love of animal-baiting, they more than redeemed themselves by their wonderful work in the theatre. Taking from the Middle Ages the rather crude miracle plays and moralities, they fashioned drama into the unsurpassed form of Shakespeare's masterpieces. The Elizabethans transformed not only what was acted, but also how and where the plays were given, and for that the whole world owes them a heavy debt.

Partly because the power of the medieval Church was declining, and partly perhaps because people were becoming a little tired of the repetition of the miracle plays, 'interludes,' the first step towards the real drama as we know it, began to be played. They were short, one-act comedies or farces, dealing with real people, and usually acted in wealthy men's halls on a portable stage with a backcloth. Sometimes the back of the stage was divided into compartments, each with a separate curtain, to represent the different houses of the characters in the play. Often these recesses bore a label so that there should be no mistake among the audience as to where an actor had gone or who he was. As they demanded little equipment and few properties, the interludes could be played most satisfactorily by the travelling companies in the rectangular inn-yards with the audience crowding on the cobbled floor or round the galleries.

But the interludes did not satisfy the crowd for long any more than the miracles had done, so that through the writings of such men as Kyd, Nicholas Udall, Peele, Greene, and Marlowe the play grew to the stature of *Macbeth* or *Hamlet*. Many of these early works were in the horror class, leaving the stage at the end strewn with corpses, poisoned, stabbed, strangled, or boiled in oil, but they were a definite stage in the development towards the great things to come.

By 1576 drama had outgrown the portable trestle-stage in noblemen's houses and inn-yards, and the first real theatre was built at Shoreditch, in London, with the rather unoriginal name of The Theatre. Because the Government was afraid that the crowding of people together to see plays would result in the spread of the plague, to say nothing of keeping honest, hard-working apprentices and craftsmen from their labour, The

Theatre was built well outside the City, where the magistrates had no authority to close it or interfere with the performances.

So successful was the new venture that others soon followed—the Swan, the Fortune, the Hope, and most famous of all, the Globe. These were all built near the bear- and bull-baiting pits at Southwark, so forming a kind of sixteenth-century Battersea playground for the growing city of London.

The big public theatres of Elizabethan London seem to have been a cross between a galleried inn-yard and the Roman theatre. They were either circular or octagonal in shape, and unroofed, though the galleries which ran right round were thatched. The plays could be given, of course, only during daylight, and usually took place in the afternoon. To advertise that a performance was to be given that day a flag decorated with the symbol of the theatre fluttered from a pole on the roof of the building all the morning.

The stage itself, either rectangular or slightly tapering, jutted out into the floor-space, and was partially roofed in. At the back, where our present-day scenery would be, was a wall into which was built a gallery, and, following the Roman pattern, three doors.

The centre doorway, much larger than the others and curtained, led to a smaller stage behind the main one, but still visible to most of the audience. This could be used when the action of the play moved to an inner room, or if necessary, with the curtains raised, both large and small stages could represent one larger acting-area.

In a similar manner the gallery running above the stage was used for acting when the play called for a balcony or bedroom-window, or perhaps a mountain scene. Trumpeters and other musicians of the theatre also used the balcony, as on occasion did the public, though they must have had a most peculiar view of the performance.

In the floor of the stage were trapdoors which could probably be raised or lowered to allow demons to make entrance or exit. Ghosts, too, often spoke from underground, and the open trap served admirably in a graveyard scene. Similarly, in the roof above the stage was an opening through which scenery or actors could be lowered on ropes by machinery when ascents to, or descents from, Heaven were called for.

With such a large stage, of course, curtains were impracticable, so that apart from the inner stage, the whole acting-space was on view the whole time, and the audience watched the comings and goings of the

The Theatre

players. Partly for this reason, scenery and properties were kept to a minimum—a throne representing a palace room, or a crucifix a church. For more difficult settings, such as outdoor scenes, the audience were usually told by one of the actors, "This is a battle-field," or "This is a forest."

The actors were all male, women's parts being played by youths with unbroken voices. This meant, unfortunately, that the boys had had no great experience on the stage, and as a result the dramatists usually made their female parts fairly simple. It was only a most exceptional boy who had the ability to act such parts as Lady Macbeth or Cleopatra.

Besides having little or no scenery, the actors had to struggle against the lack of costumes, for whatever period of history the play dealt with, the performers wore their ordinary clothes. Only a few special characters, such as archbishops and priests, Romans or Arabs, wore robes to indicate who they were.

The audiences grew rapidly as the professional acting companies replaced the amateurs of the miracle plays, and as more and more plays poured from the pens of the dramatists. They stood either on the ground round three sides of the jutting-out stage, or, for a higher payment, sat in the galleries. At the end of Elizabeth I's reign the most wealthy or important actually sat on stools on the stage, much to the actors' annoyance.

The groundlings, or those who stood, were usually of the rougher type, and, like the spectators at the bear- and cock-pits, were traditionally noisy, not hesitating to show their disapproval of an actor or a play. They chewed fruit and pies, cracked nuts, and no doubt, if bored, drank from bottles and leather flasks they had brought.

While it is of these public theatres that we generally think when talking of the stage in the times of Elizabeth I, there were at the same time a few 'private' theatres which seem to have been much more like our modern ones. They were rectangular, roofed buildings with a stage at one end, probably running right across the rather narrow hall. As the place was enclosed, artificial light in the shape of dim, flickering banks of candles suspended from the ceiling, and perhaps more along the front of the stage as footlights, gave a ghostly illumination. No doubt certain scenes from *Hamlet* would have been most effective in such surroundings.

The scenery in the private theatres was much more elaborate, and consisted of a backcloth, usually painted with a picture of a street or forest-path in perspective, in front of which were 'solid' buildings of canvas and wood. These merged with the backcloth to give the impression that the whole thing was three-dimensional.

Admission to this type of theatre was rather more expensive and selective than to the public, or open, theatres, and one hopes the behaviour there was better. They were usually run by boy actors, although Shakespeare's company sometimes had a winter season of plays in them.

Yet even the private theatres were perhaps too rough for the fastidious Court and nobles, so that the lords and ladies devised their own amateur drama called Masques, which took place in the halls of the great mansions and palaces. Certain of the courtiers dressed in elaborate costumes, and in a most extravagantly decorated setting acted a simple story, usually concerned with the life and loves of gods and godesses. Formal dancing and recitation formed a large part of the show, which was really designed as a display of colour, lighting, and spectacular scenery and dresses rather than a serious play.

After the death of the Queen, who like her father, Henry VIII, loved to take part, the masques became even more popular and magnificent, the most famous architects being commissioned to make the scenery, the greatest poets to write the poetry, and the most celebrated musicians to compose the music. Though fifty years later the masque had disappeared, the machinery and tricks used in it were afterwards adopted by the ordinary theatre so that what was originally the pastime of a very few eventually helped to increase the pleasure of the many.

Throughout the Middle Ages the homes of the people had been largely shelters—places for eating and sleeping—and much of the recreation of the people had taken place out of doors. This is not surprising when one considers the lofty, draughty, stone manor-houses and castles of the nobles, and the poor wattle-and-daub hovels of the cottagers. During the sixteenth century the increasing prosperity of the country led to a general improvement in the dwellings of rich and poor alike, and they became much more comfortable. The furniture became less stark, and the rooms smaller and warmer, so there was much more temptation to take entertainments at home. Indoor amusements, therefore, began to develop rapidly, and among them Dancing, Music, Card-playing, and Reading were perhaps most popular.

For centuries the English had enjoyed Dancing, but never before in history had it taken such a hold on all classes of society as it did in the

Tudor period. Country folk kept their traditional steps, many of which still survive to this day. There were the Roundel (a ring dance), the Hey, Cushion Dance, Hunting of the Fox, Sellinger's Round, the jigs, and one—a slow, mournful measure—called the Dumps, from which no doubt we get the expression "down in the dumps." In addition, there was the Morris Dance, performed by six men in costumes, sometimes with blackened faces and sometimes dressed as Robin Hood and his men, to the sound of bells carried on their arms and legs.

Some of the country dances were adapted for use at Court and other noble assemblies: one such was the Brawl, which apparently lived up to its name very often. But usually the upper classes thought more highly of French or Italian steps such as the Pavane (a slow, stately dance in which the couples moved forward two paces then back two), the Galliard, or Sink-a-pace (a lively step), the Coranto (a hopping step), and the Volte, or Lavolta, in which the dancers leapt high into the air, sometimes bursting their clothes, which were not at all suited to such violent exercises.

While Dancing needed space as well as opportunity, Music did not, and to be unable to play some instrument or other, or at least to be incapable of singing a part from sight, was considered to show considerable lack of social training. Music was everywhere, and English composers such as Byrd, Morley, Dowland, and Tallis were famous over the whole of the known world.

Every house worthy of the name had some instrument on which any member of the family or any caller could show his skill. There were the lutes—beautiful, guitar-like instruments; several different viols, rather like our violin, viola, and cello; recorders and hautboys (oboes); virginals —the forerunner of the piano—and even the humble bagpipes and pipe and drum. Every barber's shop would have at least one instrument hanging on the wall for customers to play while waiting for their beards to be trimmed, their hair to be cut, or minor ailments treated. The couple who to-day 'drop-in' for a hand of bridge or to watch the serial on the television would, in Elizabeth I's time, have called to complete the consort of viols (usually two treble, two tenor, and two bass) for the latest piece of music by one of the popular composers. Those who for some reason could not play would gather in groups to sing rounds and catches or the unaccompanied madrigals and balletts, this last type of song having the popular 'fa-la' chorus.

Music at home

All over the country, in the street, at the feast and fair, but more especially in the home, music sounded, and although there were professional musicians, it was the amateur, the man who sang or played because it was his hobby, from whom most of the melody arose.

Among what we should call indoor games there is no doubt that Card-playing made the greatest progress during the sixteenth century. Introduced from the Continent in the fourteenth or fifteenth centuries, cards made relatively slow progress until the reign of the Tudor kings, when the possibilities they held for gambling or mere entertainment were realized. The names of the games themselves have a delightful ring, though the details of play of many of them are lost. Maw and Primero were among the favourites, and we read that in 1575 Elizabeth I won £28 from Lord North at Maw and £33 at Primero, both on the same day. No doubt the noble lord found it good policy to allow his sovereign to win. Other games played were Cribbage, Picquet (both played to-day), Ruffe, Trumpe, Slam, Gleeke, New-cut, Swigg, Loadam, Putt, Post and Pair, Bone-ace, Seven Cards, One and Thirty, Anaken, Primfisty, and My Sow hath pigged. The very names themselves of some of the games sound criminal, and fit completely with the low, stifling, gambling-dens where many of them were played.

After Card-playing perhaps the most popular indoor game of adults was Chess, which was played by both men and women much more than it is to-day. The introduction of printing no doubt had some hand in this as one of Caxton's first books was on the rules and tactics of Chess. The game itself seems to have been little different from our own, and the mental exercise it demanded satisfied most of the learned, so the complicated and freakish Rithomomachy declined rapidly.

Draughts, the poor relation of Chess, which had been played steadily and quietly through the Middle Ages, and which had been regarded as an inferior sort of game suitable for children and ladies, suddenly began to grow in importance. Under the old rules no one was forced to take an opponent's piece if he did not wish to do so, and the introduction at the beginning of the sixteenth century of the modern rule, by which capture is compulsory, made the game much more interesting. With the penalty of huff hanging over their heads, players concentrated much more, so that learned mathematicians even considered Draughts not beneath their notice as a change from Chess.

For those whose brain-power was not equal to the more difficult

games a favourite indoor pastime was Shove-groat. This was identical
with our Shove-halfpenny, and consisted of a table or board with a
number of parallel lines about an inch wide scratched on it. A coin—
an Edward VI shilling was the great favourite in the second half of the
century—was placed slightly overhanging the edge of the table, parallel
with the scratched lines, and tapped smartly with the palm of the hand

Shove-groat

or ball of the thumb, the object being to slide the coin in between each
pair of lines in turn. Perhaps as in the modern game the groat had to be
placed three times in each 'bay' to complete that particular pair of lines.
Although no involved planning of tactics is required as in Chess or even
Draughts, Shoffe-grotte, as the Elizabethans called it, demanded
considerable skill and constant practice. As it is to-day, it was a favourite
game in inns and taverns.

With the steady class of tradesmen, Backgammon still retained its
popularity; Dicing too kept its following among a very different section
of the community because the dice could be carried in the pocket ready
for any idle moment.

G

Troule-in-madame was a simple game recommended for ladies on wet afternoons, and consisted merely of rolling small metal or wooden balls into holes made in the end of a bench. A variation of this called Trunks, or Pigeon-holes, substituted numbered arches in an upright board across the bench for the holes.

Reading, for the first time, must be considered a serious form of recreation in the sixteenth century. Crudely illustrated and quaintly spelled books and pamphlets poured from the printing-presses, and although the majority were concerned either with politics or religion, there were a great number on subjects more appealing to the mass of the people. There were books on farming for the countryman, on cookery and household matters for the womenfolk, on Angling, Hunting, Falconry for the sportsman, on Archery and Swordsmanship, accounts of voyages and unusual happenings, such as the birth of three-legged calves, volumes of poetry, and books of what are described as "merry jests and tales." These volumes of jokes read to-day often seem either pointless or crude, but apart from the descriptions of travel to distant lands, many of which must have risen from a voyage of the mind rather than of the body, they were really the only books of fiction. Even then, the "merry jests" were often anecdotes of famous people, and there was nothing to correspond with the modern novel or even short story. By one method or another, a good proportion of the population was able to read, and this sounded the death-knell of the travelling minstrel who had made his living telling stories and news, and singing ballads, to the illiterate and bookless people of the Middle Ages.

But if the Tudors lost the delight of the wandering newsmonger they found a new pleasure of which the medieval folk could not have dreamed, for soon after 1565 the New World made its first contribution to the recreation of the Old in the form of Smoking. From the very first crossing of the Atlantic, the European sailors had marvelled at the peculiar habits of the natives of burning the dried leaves of a certain plant in a tube and inhaling the smoke. No doubt many mariners during the seventy years or so after Columbus's discovery tried this for themselves when they visited the Americas and the West Indies, but it was not until the 1570's that the habit began in earnest in England. Even then it was not for pleasure but for medical reasons, as the fumes of the burning Nicotiana leaves were said to cure almost all diseases from rheumatism to boils.

Probably, too, these first tobaccos were from inferior plants, badly cured and very bitter, and it was not until a party of colonists sent out by Sir Walter Ralegh returned in 1585 that Smoking really began to make any advances.

Besides much better leaves, the travellers brought back a new device—the clay pipe—which made 'drinking' tobacco a much easier operation. Soon, led by Ralegh, many men and women at Court were puffing clay and silver pipes, though right from the start Smoking has had a noisy and powerful opposition. From the Court downward through society, and from the returning colonists upward, Smoking swept like wildfire through England, and became a recreation which four hundred years later can claim more followers than any other with perhaps the exception of Reading.

While the younger people no doubt delighted in Smoking, and indeed in all the new pastimes of the age, there is a strong tendency for children's games to be played century after century with very little change. Many pastimes of the Middle Ages or even earlier are still played happily to-day—Hopscotch, Blind Man's Buff, Hot Cockles, ring and chasing games, for example, are as important in the twentieth century as they were in the fifteenth. So the Tudor children played in much the same way as their great-great-grandparents in the thirteenth and fourteenth centuries had done, but owing to the number of books that were being printed in the sixteenth century, more of the childish amusements have been left on record for us. As civilization progresses too, adults' games of one generation are considered suitable only for children in the next generation, and the young Elizabethan inherited many games which the rather childlike grown-ups of Middle Ages had enjoyed at their festivals.

To judge from the number of times it is mentioned, Barley Break, or the Last Couple in Hell, must have been the favourite of the day, whole villages, old and young, sometimes taking a half-holiday to play this game. A rectangular field or patch of ground was divided into three equal strips by a line scratched on the ground or by sticks on the edges, and into each third a couple, usually a boy and girl, holding hands, was placed. The centre strip was Hell, and the couple there had, without breaking hands, to catch one of the couples in the other two sections. Those being chased could, if hard-pressed, break hands and run separately, but were not allowed to leave their third of the field. When one couple was caught it changed places, went to Hell, and became the chasers. The game ended when the third couple had been tagged and they were left in Hell.

Barley Break makes a good addition to the list of 'tag' games for playing in the playground or park, and previous agreement between those being chased on tactics when being hotly pursued can make the chase much more difficult for those in Hell.

King by your Leave, the old game in which one person stood on a hillock, tree-stump, log, or any other raised vantage-point, chanting:

> I'm the King of the Castle,
> Get out you dirty rascal,

as he repelled any attempt to dislodge him, is described in Elizabeth I's reign, but it is a poor and rather rough sport. This is still seen occasionally on the beach where the flush of holiday enthusiasm and discarded sandcastle prompts the rhyme, but Drawing the Dun out of the Mire, another early game, seems to have disappeared completely—and no wonder.

A large log of wood was dragged into the room to represent the dun, or cart-horse. Two players jumped forward in an attempt to lift it, calling out, "The dun is in the mire" (The horse is in the mud). When they could not do so one player after another joined in the struggle until the wood was lifted clear of the floor. The 'fun' now began: by nods, winks, or pre-arranged plans, groups of 'players' contrived to drop their end or side of the log to make it fall on the toes of the others. There was no scoring or time-limit for the game, the end coming only, one supposes, when toes and knees would take no more punishment.

So with these and all the other known and forgotten medieval running, fighting, and guessing games the Tudor children amused themselves in their all-too-short childhood, for work came very early. Perhaps it was for this reason that few actual 'things' were created for children's recreation: almost all of their amusements demanded no equipment apart from sturdy limbs and sound senses. Children were to be seen and not heard, and were important only because they would one day be adults. Their clothes were miniature replicas of their parents'; their games, other than those they could make for themselves, were largely their parents'. Two years before the sixteenth century closed, however, came a faint sign that the child would one day come into his own: from Italy came the Game of Goose, the father, grandfather, and great-grandfather of nearly all the thousands of board games that amuse children all over the world.

The game consisted of a card on which was printed a large spiral track, often in the form of a snake, of 63 squares. Two dice were used, and the counters were moved according to the throws from the tail (1) to the head (63). Fourteen of the squares bore the picture of a goose, and if a counter landed on one of these it moved on the same number of squares given by the last throw again and again until it reached a space without a goose.

Other squares bore penalties: on 19, which had a picture of an inn, the player missed two throws; on 42, a maze, he went back to 30; at 52, prison, he waited for the next person to arrive at that square, and then changed places: on 58, a skull, the player went back to the beginning.

Simple though it was, it was something completely novel and unlike any other board game in existence. The principle is so well known now that it seems impossible that no one had thought of it before. Yet they had not, and this is a sign that in recreation, as in so many other aspects of life, Europe was beginning to wake up after centuries of sleeping.

CHAPTER V

The Seventeenth Century

IT is not often that recreation is able to alter the course of history, but entertainment, or rather the lack of it, probably helped in the overthrow of Oliver Cromwell and his sober-minded Commonwealth, and in the return of the Stuart kings. But when James I came from Scotland in 1603 only the faintest whisperings of the coming gale were heard in prosperous, wealthy England.

Throughout the reign of Elizabeth I the Puritans had been growing in power, and yearly their gloomy warnings about the fate of those who took part in any amusement reached an ever-widening audience. While the Puritans frowned on recreation at any time as being wasteful and wicked, it was the traditional Sunday games that they singled out for the most violent attacks. After most of the holidays in honour of the saints had disappeared Sunday was the only regular time throughout the year when the labourer could enjoy himself. James I, worried by the attacks being made on his subjects' amusements, therefore issued in 1618 his famous declaration usually known as the first "Book of Sports" which had to be read in every church in the country. To prevent the people of England being tempted to change back to the old religion which allowed games on the Sabbath, and so that they would be made fit for war by the Sunday exercise, he urged every person, after attending morning service, to indulge in "lawful recreation" such as Dancing, Leaping, Vaulting, Archery, and other such harmless recreations. Only Bear- and Bull-baiting and theatrical shows were to be banned on the Lord's Day. May Games, Whitsun-ales (the Church-ales of the Middle Ages were now celebrated usually on Whit Sunday), Morris-dancing, and maypoles, all of which the Puritans discouraged, were, James said, not only permissible but also to be encouraged. A final order, and one of which it seems no one took any notice, was that poor people must not play Bowls, for by this time bowling-alleys had acquired a very bad reputation. "Three things besides the bowls are thrown away there," said one Stuart sports-writer, "money, sense, and curses."

Apart from among their own followers and in districts where they were in a majority, the Puritans could do little about the "Book of Sports." They raged and preached against it, but the usual jollifications still took place with the added zest of poking fun at the black-coated Fathers who looked on so disapprovingly. Yet the time was rapidly approaching when the Puritans were to have their full revenge in the joyless years of the Commonwealth.

Meanwhile the old games from the medieval and Tudor times were enjoyed with little change, and all the former vigour. The countryman hunted in the woods and chases which every year shrank in size before the onslaught of agriculture. The stag was still the king of the forest, but his subjects dwindled in number with the trees, so that the humbler but no less exciting hare was hunted more and more. Every year too saw some improvement in the safety, design, and accuracy of the musket which gradually took more and more of the fowling from the hawks. The draining of marshes and fens in the interest of farming caused the number of herons and other waterbirds to dwindle, and this too helped in the decline of the falcon, for the swampy river-banks were the favourite haunt of the falconer. But the old sport was by no means dead: the Duke of Bedford still paid his chief falconers £120 a year, while his huntsmen received only £16.

The nobility kept up their round of amusement: they hunted in the woods, acted in, or watched, elaborate masques, went to the private theatres to see the plays of Mr Shakespeare, danced, or played Tennis. James, coming from Scotland where the game was already well established, introduced the Court to Golf, but failed to interest more than a few of his friends, and in England at least Golf was to remain a simple country game of knocking a wooden ball round a field with a knobbly stick for nearly another three centuries.

Little enough entertainment could be bought ready-made in either town or country so that when the date for the annual fair approached it is little wonder that the district for miles around buzzed with a thrill of expectancy. Most parts of England were within reach of at least one of the great occasions, and as it lasted for several days or even a week there was plenty of opportunity for folk from quite distant villages to pay a visit by coach, on horseback, or even on foot, to squander the few shillings they could ill afford on worthless trifles and brief delirious glimpses of the great outside world.

All through the Tudor period the importance of the great medieval fairs such as Sturbridge, near Cambridge, and St Bartholomew, at Smithfield, for serious trading had been declining. As shops and manufacturers increased in number, and as ships travelled from the corners of the world more swiftly and more certainly, there was no longer any necessity for the citizen to wait for the fair to buy his needles, glass, ribbons, or wine. Even in the Middle Ages, when everything not made locally had to be bought when the pedlars and merchants held their annual market, entertainers had accompanied the salesmen from town to town, and in the seventeenth century these became increasingly important. True, there was still buying and selling, but much of it had changed from the bread-and-butter clothing and shoes and tools to unnecessary luxuries such as ornaments, toys, trinkets, and useless fancy goods. Some of the provincial fairs, however, continued to sell large numbers of horses and huge quantities of wool and hops, but even here the customers hurried through their serious bargaining to hasten to the more enjoyable part of the field where the raucous amusements were in full blast.

The fair itself was laid out in a huge field or open space like a miniature town with streets of booths, tents, and stalls leading to squares where various contests were taking place. Up and down the grassy roads the owners of the booths burst their leather lungs in competition with the bellowing pedlars, the wailing musicians, and the general screaming mob of pleasure-seekers. The toysellers with their simple dolls, tops, bats, rattles, and toy weapons carried on a noisy and bitter rivalry for the children's custom with the musical-instrument merchants whose stalls were heavy with fiddles, trumpets, Jews'-harps, drums, and bird-warblers. Both pitted themselves against the wandering sellers of hobby-horses and the old women with their baskets of very cheap gingerbread figures.

For the hungry—and fighting and jostling with the crowd up and down the lengthy trackways was an exhausting business—there were food stalls to satisfy every taste, but the oyster-table and the roasting-pig booth were the general favourites, followed closely by the hot-sausage and black-pudding stand. For five shillings the starving could buy a baby pig roasted whole, and wash it down with ale or beer at sixpence a bottle. Pipes of tobacco—the cheapest variety and adulterated with half its weight of coltsfoot leaves which cost nothing—were an additional attraction at threepence each.

Then, rested, full, and perhaps a little queasy after the greasy piglet and rank tobacco, out into the swirling bustle again to watch the Wrestling—one of the few free entertainments—or, if drunk enough, to make a match with the sword-and-buckler man who, like the modern boxer, challenged all comers. With the minds perhaps a little hazy, money would flow like water, and there were all too many pools into which it could run. There were the rows of booths, each, according to the busker who roared from the entrance, the best and only genuine one in the fair, with freaks, giants, midgets, and monsters; others gave displays of rope-dancing, juggling, conjuring, or trained dogs and apes who bowed for the king and made fun of France, Spain, or whoever happened to be the popular current enemy.

From here, if any money still lingered red-hot in the purse, the pleasure-seeker fought his way past the ballad singers, the pear-sellers, the mousetrap man, the tooth-puller, and the corn-cutter to the puppet shows, which were perhaps the main attraction of the fair, and to the tents where live actors performed.

The ever popular puppet shows were mainly the old miracle and morality plays with, one suspects, some very un-Biblical additions. The names of some of them—Sodom and Gomorrah, the Fall of Nineveh, the Fall of Jerusalem—hint that the more violent and less savoury episodes of the Old Testament were the favourites. Classical legends were also shown, but perhaps the most popular of all were the topical plays— *The Gunpowder Plot*, soon after the real event, was given nine times in one afternoon, and *The Revolt of the Norwich Apprentices*, again a news item, nearly as many.

If the money-bag contained any change at all at this stage—and the pickpockets, tricksters, and cheats who thronged the fair made this very unlikely—there were presents to be bought from the stalls laden with purses, pouches, pipes, pins, and ornaments. Then, if one was not tired of deafening babel, there was always a less crowded corner where a wandering bagpipe-player or fiddler would, for a copper, scrape up a tune for general dancing.

All this was but once a year: on the other days the workman and apprentices in the towns still cracked nuts and shouted encouragement in the pit at the open public theatres, screamed at the Bull- and Bear-baitings, betted furiously at the cockpits, or journeyed the short distance to join their country brothers in the rural sports of Wrestling, Archery, Tossing the Sledgehammer or log of wood, Quoits, Skittles, or Bowls. The Dressing of the Maypole early in the morning with the dancing and games which followed, and the Christmas festivities, were still the high-lights of the year for most of the country as the thunderclouds of the coming civil war piled up over Westminster.

Then came the storm of six years' fighting, the execution of King Charles I, and the coming into being of the dark twelve years of the Puritan Commonwealth. Every one realized, some with satisfaction, but most with dismay, that grim, cheerless days lay ahead.

The real theatres with live actors, which were regarded by the new Government as especially sinful, had closed in 1642, but even so, wealthy drama-lovers still managed to have shortened performances of the old plays more or less secretly in the great halls of their mansions. Word would be passed round from trusted friend to trusted friend, and probably actors from the disbanded companies were invited, disguised as guests. Even those who were not fortunate enough to have large houses managed, as people always will with something they want very much, to avoid the regulations, and in the old miracle and morality plays which had been transferred to the puppet theatres the wooden figures strutted quite openly at fairs and public gatherings.

At first Oliver Cromwell's Government was not too harsh in the matter of sports and games, but as the stricter officials took over more and more power in the different districts, dancing, games, maypole festivities, and even singing, were punished. Cards, Dicing, Bowls, and other gambling games had of course been classed as playthings of the devil and his followers since the beginning, and in one village we read of people actually being fined for walking for pleasure in the fields on Sunday.

The Puritans themselves no doubt did refrain from ungodly amuse-ments, but advice, warnings, threats, and even punishments could not stop the great mass of the people from taking part in the traditional sports in one form or another. Even the Government did not dare to interfere too much with the great fairs which, although very much toned down and without plays and the worst elements, still remained, with crowded booths, the puppet shows, and stalls. All that the prohibitions on recreation managed to do was to increase the hatred felt for the rulers and their system, and to make men long for the old free-and-easy ways of the kings again.

Yet the twelve years of the Commonwealth, with its grim, unsmiling severity, were not without their good side, especially for the next generation of children. Many of the Cavaliers and supporters of the king fled

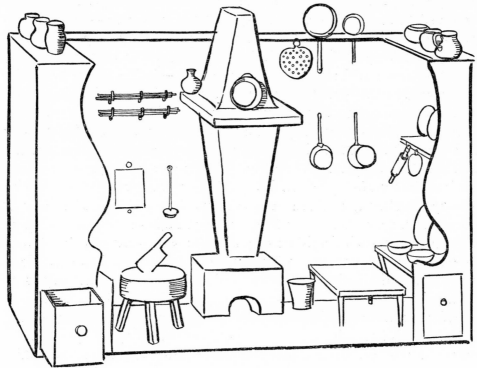

A Nuremberg kitchen

to the Continent when Charles was defeated and there saw new games, especially toys for children. Germany and France in particular were beginning to regard boys and girls, not as half-size grown-ups, but as beings in their own right and needing special amusements of their own. When in 1660 Charles II returned to England as king, his fellow-exiles brought back not only new ideas, but actual toys as well for their families, who were by then often too old for them.

For the smaller children there were rocking-horses which seem to have been popular in Germany at this time. These ranged from quite simple types consisting of two semicircular wooden rockers and a flat

board head to beautifully carved realistic steeds prancing on their curved
wooden bases with tail erect and head well back. These two models have
become traditional for English rocking-horses, for any large toyshop
to-day will show you a dozen almost identical with the first to reach this
country over three hundred years ago.

Girls, who for centuries had fared rather worse than boys in the matter
of playthings, gained more from the returning Royalists than the boys,
for exiled fathers and uncles brought back better dolls—or babies, as
they were called—and dolls' houses which were really playthings. It is
true that as early as Queen Elizabeth I's reign, and even before, tiny
human figures had been on sale at the fairs—St Bartholomew babies
were quite famous—but these were elaborately decorated with ribbons
and lace, and were most probably more often used by adults as ornaments
than played with by ordinary children. Some of the earlier 'dolls' may
have had religious connexions, for a number from the beginning of the
seventeenth century were named after saints or the Virgin Mary.

There had probably been a few dolls' houses imported before 1660 by
wealthy merchants, but these too were possibly showpieces for adults.
They were huge models, often five or six feet high and containing up to
a dozen rooms, each furnished exquisitely down to the last detail with
tablecloths, cutlery, and even flat-irons in the basement laundry. Now,
at the Restoration, miniature houses which were designed for play came
to England for the first time. The first ones were Nuremberg kitchens—
named after the town in Germany where they were manufactured—
and consisted of a single boxlike room complete with tiny stove, saucepans,
mortar and pestle, knives, chopping-block, graters, and scales. While
these were probably intended to teach the young girl the first principles
of housekeeping, which every married woman was supposed to know
however rich she was, they were soon to become pure playthings. The
kitchen soon demanded a dining-room, and so the houses expanded,
but as every item had to be made by hand, early dolls' houses were for
the very wealthy girl only. Two centuries were to pass before the ordinary
girl could have a miniature home that was more than mere make-believe.

Yet if the larger toys were not available to the majority of children
no home need have been without the Game of Goose which could be
printed on paper and sold for a few coppers. Although no specimen has
survived as early as the seventeenth century, it is quite probable that
children soon made variations of the game, for once the idea has been

Pell-mell

discovered it is easy to put different rewards and punishments on the squares.

Another simple game, again probably introduced from the Continent, was Cup and Ball. This consisted of a wooden handle, rather like an ice-cream cone, to which was fastened by a short piece of string a wooden ball. The sport consisted of jerking the ball into the air and catching it in the cup as it fell. Not very exciting, perhaps, but it has lived for three centuries, though the mechanical mind of the twentieth century demands a trigger-operated spring to launch its ball into the air.

More exciting than balls on the ends of pieces of string were the paper Kites which were introduced at the end of the century from China. Most probably these had been brought by French merchants, and gradually, with the other toys and games, found their way to England.

Every child over the age of eight, we are told, was an expert at Whist and other adult card games, but simple ones, possibly similar to Beggar-my-neighbour, were more usual for the youngest. Some special packs were made for grammar games which educated and amused at the same time—an early example of the teaching 'amusements' which were to become so popular with Victorian parents two hundred years later.

Cup and Ball

The grown-ups had not been forgotten by the returning exiles either, and the new sport of Pell-mell soon became the rage of London. In a level court, or track, made of sand covered with well-brushed, powdered cockleshell, a post rather like a gibbet was erected. From this was suspended a metal ring about a foot in diameter, the object of the game being to drive a boxwood ball through the hoop with a long-handled wooden hammer rather like a croquet-mallet. It seems to have been a rather dull game, and, apart from giving its name to Pall Mall in London, which was the site of one of the most famous grounds devoted to this sport, it has died out in its original form almost without a trace.

The Royalists who had spent their icy exile in Holland saw how much more skilful the Dutch were on their frozen canals than were the English. Soon crude skates made of bone, which had been used for so long in England, were replaced by the iron Continental pattern with the long curling fronts. But English winters in most parts of the land are unreliable, and outdoor Skating, despite the great frosts in the past, has always been a most uncertain sport here, so that it was a pleasure which touched relatively few people.

Skating

Judging by the way in which the Court and nobility threw themselves into the wild pursuit of pleasure, it seemed as if they were determined to make up for the twelve years that they had spent, sometimes in considerable hardship, away from their homeland. On their country estates they hunted wherever possible, and went shooting, often on horseback, with guns that were now becoming so accurate that we are told that they sometimes actually hit birds in the air as opposed to sitting targets. But perhaps the two most popular country pursuits of the wealthy, because no doubt they lent themselves to betting, were Paddock-coursing and Horse-racing. Both in the form they then took were new, and were a particular feature of the second half of the seventeenth century.

For Paddock-coursing a strip of grass at least a mile long and a quarter of a mile wide, enclosed by a wall or fence, was needed. At one end were the cages for the dogs, and a pen for the deer or stag to be chased. Posts were placed on the side of the track at a distance of 160 yards, a quarter of a mile, and half of a mile from the pens, and then, near the opposite end from the kennels, a ditch was dug across the course. Between the half-mile marker and the finishing-line was the pinching-post, which had to be passed by both the hunters and hunted if the race was to be allowed.

The dogs were shut in, and on a signal the deer was released. To encourage it to move quickly, a fast but gentle dog called the Teaser was let go when the deer had gone about twenty yards. When the quarry reached the 160-yard post, and was at full gallop pursued by the Teaser, the traps were lifted, and the greyhounds, who no doubt had been in a ferment of anxiety and excitement as the deer escaped, bounded down the course. If the deer was caught the owner of the victorious dog received the prize, provided the pinching-post had been reached, but if it outpaced its enemies and leapt across the ditch, beyond which the judges sat, it was safe, and was rescued. The first dog to reach the gully, or the nearest to it when the deer was saved, was judged the winner, and the bets were paid out. In a rough time this was a reasonably kindly sport, differing in principle very little from our modern greyhound-racing tracks.

For those not rich enough to possess a paddock at least a mile long hares were normally coursed in open country, and, we are told, were usually given about 240 yards start to make the sport better. It seems hard to reconcile these fair and humane ideals with the savage and in-human Bull-, Bear-, and Horse-baiting which were still carried on up and down the country.

Of all the introductions in the field of recreation made in the seventeenth century, without a doubt the most important was Horse-racing. There must have been racing on horseback before this time of course, for it is impossible in a time when every one of any wealth rode for the words "Beat you to yonder tree" not to have been said in challenge. But to the Stuarts must go the credit of the first organized race-meetings, though these were held on any suitable flat space, and were open to all who wished to watch.

The horses were Turkish stallions, if obtainable, but Richard Blome complained, in 1686, that the Turks were so unwilling to part with their steeds that usually only second-rate ones came to England. Spanish or Barbary animals, normally used as riding-horses, were employed if the real racers were not available.

Horse-racing

The jockeys were advised to dress in tight trousers and jackets of coloured silk—quilted for warmth—with a cap tied on their heads. Good sharp spurs were essential, and not only for use on the horse, either.

The actual races were run in three or four heats, with half an hour between each event to allow the horses to be rubbed down and to cool off. The same horses ran in each heat, the winner being the animal which gained the most points in the whole series. A post was erected some two hundred yards from the finishing-line, and any rider who had not reached this point by the time the winner had reached the end of the course was considered outclassed and took no part in the following heats.

The jockeys, who sat bolt upright on their mounts and did not crouch in the fashion of modern jockeys, were weighed both before and after the race to make sure they did not cheat by throwing away any of the weights they had been forced to carry to make the horses' burdens equal.

There does seem to be something in Horse-racing which draws out the worst side in men, for right from the beginning of its career it attracted besides the genuine sportsmen and horse-lovers, rogues, cheats, sharpers, and those in search of money without working for it. All of these flocked to the race-meetings to trick or rob the simpletons of their money, and then to lose it themselves in gambling on the horses. Having little interest in the races except as a means of getting rich, this riff-raff has through the ages brought the sport into disrepute in the eyes of many people.

Back in the city the well-to-do and the middle classes had a brand new form of entertainment in the coffee-houses, the first of which was opened in London in the middle of the century, and which gained rapidly in popularity after the restoration of the King. Inns had of course flourished from earliest times, but the coffee-house, serving the newly introduced coffee, tea (without milk or sugar), and chocolate, were on a much higher level than the noisy, brawling taverns. Although these coffee-houses were to develop in the next century into the great clubs, at first they offered no more than refreshment and the opportunity to talk and discuss matters of the day over a long clay pipe of the ever more popular tobacco.

Perhaps a coffee-house here and there may have had a billiard-table to amuse its patrons and to attract custom, but if not there were few towns without one public room where the game might be played. The seventeenth-century Billiards was played on a rectangular board covered with green cloth and fitted with six pockets as in the modern game, but there most of the similarity between the two ends. Apart from the completely

Billiards

different method of play, the dead-level surface of the modern table was hard to find as the old wooden tables warped, leaving hollows and hummocks which were no small advantage to a player familiar with them.

On the table, a few inches from one end, stood a metal or ivory peg called the king, and at the other a bridge rather like a croquet-hoop. Each player had an ivory ball and an ivory-tipped, tapering cue, either end of which could be used for play. The balls were hit up and down the table by the players alternately, the skill being in placing the ball so that one's opponent's next stroke was either useless or caused him to lose a point. These points could be gained or lost in a number of complicated ways—touching the king with a ball but not knocking it over, for example, won one, whereas knocking the king down, hitting the ball into a pocket or off the table, lost one. Rather harshly, dragging one's sleeve across the cloth when playing forfeited a point as did dropping tobacco-ash on the table. Five points made a game in daylight, but after dark, by candlelight, it was only three—a fact which makes us realize just how gloomy even public buildings must have been three hundred years ago, and how difficult it was to score.

A variation of Billiards called Trucks does not seem to have survived, and to judge by its description it is little loss. The table was similar to that for Billiards, but was longer, and had twenty-six pockets, three in each short side and ten on each long one. The king and the bridge, in this game called Sprigg and Arglio, were fixed rigidly to the table, and the balls, made of ivory and about the size of tennis-balls, were struck with an iron-tipped cue. Truly it sounds a most formidable sport.

Rather surprisingly, the theatres took a long time to regain the popularity they had had before the Commonwealth, for the Puritan propaganda about their sinfulness seems to have had great effect on the mass of the people. Those which did open immediately the king returned were patronized almost entirely by the Court and the nobility, and as the audience and the players often knew each other personally, the pieces written for the performance were full of local scandal, private jokes, and gossip. So friendly were the intimate theatres that the king actually lent some of his clothes to the actors for use on the stage.

Although most of the plays given were by Ben Jonson, Beaumont, Fletcher, and Shakespeare, a new group of dramatists was beginning to write pieces more to the taste of the wealthy patrons. Many of these

Restoration plays were clever, witty, and sophisticated, and throw a brilliant light on the manners of the upper classes. Unfortunately, the morals of the Court often left much to be desired, so that some of the drama of the late seventeenth century would cause lifted eyebrows if given to-day. The actual performances on the stage probably improved too, for women began more and more to take over the female parts from the young male actors.

The theatres themselves too were beginning to look more like modern ones inside, the main difference being in the stage which still projected forward into what now would be the orchestra-pit and the front rows of the stalls.

The scenery became much more flexible as well, and consisted of painted sheets of wood and canvas which slid in grooves in the floor of the stage. Half of each scene was on one side of the stage and half on the other, so that when a new background was required a pair of stage-hands pushed the halves in from each side until they met. As the curtain was raised at the beginning of the performance and not lowered until the end, the scene-shifting was done in full view of the audience and the players. The candle-snuffers too, who during the play trimmed the wicks of the footlights and the candelabra, walked on the stage regardless of the action taking place there, so that at times, with actors, scene-shifters, and candle-snuffers all wandering to and fro, the plot must have been most confusing. However, it was usually arranged that a song or interlude covered this period of unusual activity.

Apart from the straight plays in the theatre, a new form of entertainment from Italy, called the *commedia dell'arte*, was occasionally seen in London. This was the real forerunner of the pantomime, and consisted of a whole series of plays each with the same characters. There was always a pair of lovers, a man and woman dressed in the costume of the period, who were attended by their servants, Harlequin and Colombine. Harlequin always wore a costume with coloured patches, and Columbine an elaborate white dress. Like most of the characters in the play, both wore masks. Pierrot was another simple-minded-servant character, always in trouble, and dressed in the loose white costume and ruff that is familiar to us as that of the seaside entertainer. Pantaloon was always an old man with a hooknosed mask, a long black gown, and slippers, and who was invariably cheated of his money. Perhaps the most interesting character of all was Punchinello, or Punch, a rascally coward who wore a hooked nose, a hunched back, and swaggering costume. He, of course, took to the puppet theatre in the eighteenth century, and became the Punch of Punch and Judy.

The *commedia dell'arte* players were highly skilled for they had no set lines to learn. They would be told the story of the play, and then they made the words up as they went along, but as the stories were probably all very similar, they kept a stock of jokes to suit, and padded them out with topical references.

The theatre and the coffee-house were born in, and developed in, the city—perhaps because of the city. By the seventeenth century London in particular had grown to such an extent that it was no longer easy for the working-people to escape from the streets and houses and, above all, the smoke to the countryside. The wealthy merchant or nobleman could retire to his house in the country for hunting, but after the gay life of the town the loneliness of woods and fields and moorland soon became boring, especially for the ladies. To enable society to enjoy the delights of the country and the company and life of the town at the same time, a new entertainment was created in the form of the spas, or watering-places.

As early as the reign of Elizabeth I a few doctors had rediscovered the fact that the water of some districts contained valuable chemicals which helped to cure certain diseases. As the seventeenth century progressed more and more people were sent to such towns as Bath and Epsom to drink or bathe in the waters for the sake of their health. As water as a medicine was far more pleasant than the majority of the fearful mixtures made by doctors of the period, the spas prospered, and inns were built to house the invalids, real and imaginary.

Bathing even in the naturally hot waters at Bath grew monotonous after a few days, and when the spa water was used merely for drinking boredom set in much earlier so that the patients organized balls or card games among themselves to pass the time. Travelling actors, conjurers, musicians, and showmen with an eye to business might set up their booths when passing to entertain the visitors, and this in turn attracted more people from the cities who were not really ill at all, but were going to the spas for the amusements. The whole thing was like a snowball rolling downhill—more visitors attracted better entertainment, and the better entertainment in turn brought even more visitors.

In the Stuart times this took place only on a small scale, but in the next century visiting the watering-places was a major recreation, and, with a shift of emphasis from the inland spa to the seaside, has remained one ever since.

The poor man in the town, however, had no share in the fun of Bath or Epsom: apart from Sunday and one or two religious feasts such as Christmas Day, he had no holidays even if he had had the money. For him, gambling in one form or another was the chief amusement.

Cockpits, bear-pits, and bull-pits were always crowded with the usual screaming mass, betting furiously on the outcome of the various contests; inns and other establishments were thronged with card- and dice-players, usually on the lookout for a fool to cheat.

Many of these card games were ridiculously simple and demanded nothing but luck and a long purse. In one very popular example each of the players named a card whereon the dealer turned up the pack one by one, the person whose card first appeared collecting money from all the others. While this was probably fair, even if foolish, among friends, playing with a stranger was fatal—all too often the dealer was an expert card manipulator who could have made a fortune honestly as a conjuror.

Dicing too was a trap for the unwary: false dice could be bought for eight shillings a set, true ones for sixpence—a reflection on the values of right and wrong in some quarters. The ingenuity used in making trick dice too would, if used in some legal pursuit, have brought the faker a fortune: hollowed-out cubes were filled with quicksilver to make them fall in a certain way, but as this method could be easily detected, the more clever rogues drilled a tiny hole in one corner, and when playing inserted a pig's bristle with a short length protruding. This ensured that the dice always rolled to a high number when the cheat was throwing, and, by changing the bristle secretly to the opposite corner, to a low one when the victim's turn came.

While one had to move in certain circles to enjoy the thrill of gambling with dice, cards, or animal-fighting, the big lotteries which began towards the end of the century were open to all, men, women, and childen. Some of these sweepstakes, the book lotteries, were obviously designed with the upper and more intellectual classes in mind, for all the prizes consisted of expensively bound volumes of classics. The first prize in one such draw, for example, consisted of an illustrated Bible, value £25; a Virgil, £5; an *Iliad*, £5; an *Odyssey*, £5; and Aesop's *Fables*, £3. After this there were scores of prizes gradually decreasing in value down to a single book worth

£1. Tickets for these were five shillings each, and if a gambler bought five at once, all of which drew blanks, he was given one book as a consolation prize. If, feeling rash, he bought eight tickets and again drew all blanks he could choose between an *Iliad*, an Aesop, and an *Odyssey*.

For those less wealthy or less educated the penny lottery was a far greater attraction: the first prize here was £1000 in cash, a very large sum in those days, and tradition says that the winning card was given by its owner, a poor boy, in exchange for a crust of bread before the draw took place.

So England amused itself at the end of the seventeenth century— the majority of people enjoying the same recreations as their forefathers in the Middle Ages had done. Few realized in 1699 that before the next century closed England would be the possessor of an Empire ranging from India to Canada, and that the old medieval farming way of life would have almost gone, sweeping vast numbers of countrymen into the unfamiliar inferno of the city slums that sprang to life as the land writhed in the throes of the Industrial Revolution. The last century of what has come to be known as the traditional Merry England had closed, and none knew it.

CHAPTER VI

The Eighteenth Century

AS the reigns of Anne and the first three Georges rolled on towards the nineteenth century, the seeds of many of our present recreations, which had lain so long dormant in the soil of the centuries, began to germinate. Some, such as Cricket, Horse-racing, seaside holidays, and especially children's toys, were by the year 1799 well-established and strongly flourishing growths.

Although by our modern standards there was much that was coarse, brutal, and cruel in the amusements of the period, there was a kindness and humanity in the air which forced some of the earlier pastimes to disappear or to change in form to something less harsh. The advances in science and engineering made other pastimes obsolete, while the improving conditions of roads and communications in general spread ideas throughout the country and broadened people's minds. The newspaper and the newly discovered novel brought new thoughts on entertainment to the farthest part of the land, and caused many to wonder if the savage local amusements which had been practised for centuries were right after all.

In the countryside great changes were taking place: the farming revolution hustled the old strip fields into the enclosed farms we know to-day. Thousands of peasants moved to swell the squalor in the bustling new factory towns of the North, and with the majority of countrymen now labourers on a large new farm instead of small farmers in their own right, many of the festivals connected with the land tended to disappear. Before long only Whitsun and Harvest Home were celebrated, and these together with Christmas and the local fair were the highlights of the landworkers' year.

At all of these feasts the whole village let itself go, and indulged in what were probably among the main national pastimes in the eighteenth century—eating, getting drunk, and, as a minor relief, smoking. But at the Whitsun holiday especially there were less harmful recreations. Even here much of the brutality usually associated with the countryside seems to have disappeared from the sports, many of which can still be seen to-day, though in our century they are usually regarded as games for children only.

All of the villagers able to walk would gather in the traditional field for the amusements, chattering and laughing. As the day progressed there was Sack-racing for the men who, with the bags tied round their necks, lumbered and fell for the crowd's amusement; for thrills there was the race of the blindfolded villagers running with their heavy, lumbering wheelbarrows. The energetic could enter a Jingling-match in which nine competitors with handkerchiefs over their eyes inside a roped-off enclosure tried to catch a tenth man, not blindfolded, but who had tiny bells attached to knees and elbows. If the jingler managed to evade capture for half an hour he was awarded the prize, which otherwise went to the first person to catch him. For those who had even more enthusiasm —and more ambition, for the prize was much more valuable—there was the Soaped Pig. The unfortunate animal had its tail cut off fairly short, and when it had been well soaped and was thoroughly slippery it was turned loose for the village to chase. The one who succeeded in catching the pig and holding it with one hand by its stump was given it to keep. If something less energetic was one's choice there was usually a prize of a guinea for the best whistler. The 'competitors' had to perform in front of the village funny man who, by posturing, making faces, or by any other method he chose, tried to make the whistlers laugh.

" Making ugly faces... *framed in a horse-collar..."*

Making ugly faces with one's head framed in a horse-collar was another quiet entertainment, though there were always the rude comments that some competitors started off with a marked advantage over the others.

In one corner of the field there was the Hasty Pudding eating-contest in which the greediest competed to see who could eat the largest amount

Hobby-horses . . .

and marionettes

in a given time. Near by was the Smoking-race: sometimes this was to
find the man who could smoke a pipeful of tobacco the most rapidly,
but more often—and more sensibly—to find the one who could make
one filling last the longest without relighting. For ladies only was the
Shift-race, a flat race for which the prize was traditionally the shift—
a long vest with sleeves, resembling a nightshirt, which fluttered from
the branch of a tree near the winning-post. As men sometimes had
ploughing-matches for a pair of breeches, a vigorous and skilful family
might manage to win a good part of its year's clothing and food at the
Whitsun sports.

The actual games varied, naturally, from village to village, but the
ones mentioned, together with Wrestling, Cudgel-play, and ordinary
racing formed the basis of most meetings. Some 'entertainments' such
as that in the Cotswolds where two brawny labourers, shod in heavy
boots, grasped each other's shoulders and hacked at each other's shins
until one gave in, did not, quite understandably, gain much popularity
outside their own particular area.

For the farmer and country gentleman too things had changed:
apart from a few enthusiasts and cranks, Hawking and Archery had
finally yielded to sporting-guns. Although single-barrelled and, towards
the end of the century, double-barrelled guns were reaching a fairly
high standard of accuracy and safety, they were still rather slow as a
hurried reload could be dangerous. As the gunpowder too was relatively
weak, the shot travelled slowly so that considerable skill and much
practice was needed to learn the allowance to be made for flying birds
and cross winds. Skilled sportsmen now scorned to shoot at sitting birds
as their fathers had been forced to do, and some actually placed so much
reliance on the accuracy of their weapons that they shot at single birds
in flight. The majority, however, still preferred to blaze away at a whole
flock in the hope of hitting at least one.

Hunting in the manner of the Tudors or even the earlier Stuarts
had now gone from most of England: the spread of farming had wiped
out the stag and deer in the wild state apart from a few isolated areas.
A few wealthy gentlemen tried to arrest the passage of time and progress
by having stags brought in cages to be released for hunting, but this did
not prove satisfactory. The hare, however, was plentiful, and in the wide,
open country afforded excellent sport. Although the Stuart laws forbidding anyone owning below a certain amount of property to possess

a greyhound were still in force, every villager had an animal of one sort or another. The harriers, or hare-hunters, could be as simple or as grand as one's pocket and wishes allowed; the noble on horseback, with his large pack of hounds, probably got no more enjoyment than the cottager following his mongrel lurcher on foot, coursing the hare. To give the eighteenth-century huntsman his due, he seems to have enjoyed the chase more than the mere gaining of a tasty joint for the pot, as he usually speaks with admiration of the hare that escaped.

In the North of England especially, the sport of Hunting the Fox— an animal which a few years earlier had been considered pure vermin and affording no sport at all—was becoming fashionable. This, however, was a recreation for the wealthy only, as it demanded a good stable of horses and an expensive pack of hounds. The fox travels much farther than the hare, so that Hunting involved much cross-country travel, and as the landscape had in most places been divided into fields by hedges, jumping became one of the pleasures.

The horses used for Hunting were not as fast as our modern animals, and in order to give the hunters at least a sporting chance of making a kill, the chase began very early in the morning—perhaps four o'clock— while the fox was still drowsy and heavy with his overnight feast of rabbit or poultry. A Frenchman travelling in Britain in the eighteenth century tells us in his diary that runs of fifty to sixty miles were frequent, and the horses were often so tired that they could not carry their riders back home. Then, says the gossipy Frenchman, the hunters went to the nearest inn for the night, and returned the following day. This too, of course, helped to confine the sport to the wealthy circle who had time to spare.

Actually taking place in the countryside, but attracting, as now, the majority of its support from the towns, was Horse-racing. Epsom and Newmarket quite early established themselves as favourite courses, but up and down the country were scores of local tracks—level spaces of ground marked with perhaps starting-, winning-, and distance-posts. The courses were marked only by the lines of spectators, and the enthusiasts' coaches and carriages formed the only grandstands. Many of the great races of to-day had their beginnings in the eighteenth century—the first St Leger Sweepstakes was run in the grounds of an army officer of that name in 1776, but it was not then called the St Leger; the first Oaks, the famous race for young mares, in 1779, and the first Derby Stakes at Epsom in 1780.

The horses too were becoming much finer and faster as better Arab stock was brought to England when the Turks could be persuaded to sell. The greatest racehorse of all time, Eclipse, was born in 1764, since when his descendants have won many Derbys.

But if the quality of the horses was improving, that of the riders certainly was not. While many of the mounts were ridden by their owners, there was a growing number in the hands of professional jockeys, and the behaviour of these, and indeed of the noblemen who rode their own coursers, was deplorable. During the actual race the riders often attacked each other with their whips, kicked each other, and tried to knock each other from the saddle.

Even if a jockey avoided all these hazards on the course and managed to win he was still not out of danger for frequently the winning rider was set upon by that section of the crowd which had backed the other runners. Sometimes the unfortunate man was badly injured by the angry losers before he could be rescued by his supporters.

Betting on the races was heavy and wild, and all business was conducted by word of mouth. Accounts were usually settled at a coffee-house or inn on the morning after the race, and the punishment for failing to pay one's debts was a sound horse-whipping. The law of the time did not consider this kind of assault to be a crime, so that a defaulting gambler could not appeal for legal protection, and had either to pay up or take his punishment.

As to-day, Horse-racing gathered to itself a small group of men whose activities hovered in the shadows that divide honest dealings from crime. At every meeting there were the tricksters in search of easy money which they lost just as easily in gambling themselves. There were the dicers with their weighted and false dice, but far more numerous were the card-sharpers who with marked packs, by sleight of hand, or with the assistance of confederates, relieved wealthy young noblemen of thousands of pounds or the country yokel of his shilling.

While on the country racecourse the peer and the peasant rubbed shoulders, there was little contact between them except in the way of business—betting, bribery, or brutality. Not far away, however, lord and labourer could be seen enjoying themselves as equals on the cricket-field.

From its very beginnings as an organized game in the eighteenth century Cricket has had the peculiar quality of making all men equal,

Cricket

and is easily the greatest contribution made by the wild, tempestuous century to the history of sport. As early as 1598 there is mention of a field set aside for 'Crickett' at Guildford, and in 1300 Edward I enjoyed a pastime called 'Creag,' but exactly what these games were, we do not know. It is probable that they were played with a club of some sort and a ball, for the Saxon word 'cricc' means a stick, and it is more than likely that the earlier 'Cricketts' varied widely.

However, in the south-east corner of England, probably in Kent, all these rural games of throwing balls at milking-stools and tree-stumps, catching and hitting balls with clubs, went into the melting-pot, and by 1700 something resembling modern Cricket had emerged. True, the wickets consisted of two forked sticks a foot high and up to two feet apart with a third twig laid across the tops; true, the bat was a heavy club shaped like a hockey-stick with a very thick end to prevent the ball from passing through the low wicket; and true, the ball was rolled along the ground at the batsman. But still it was a kind of Cricket.

In the early games the number of players was not definite, but in the single game, when one batsman at a time was on the field, the usual number was five a side. For the double game, in which two sets of wickets and two batsmen were used, the team was normally eleven. The batsmen could be dismissed by a catch or if the man behind the wicket could pop the ball through the hole of the wicket before the scorer had finished his run. There must have been some pretty sharp knocks, accidental and deliberate, on the 'wicket-keeper's' knuckles by batsmen struggling to get 'home.'

In the double game an over consisted of four balls, not six as to-day—probably a survival of the days when each man except the captain of the small team had one bowl each at the wicket. Two umpires, each leaning heavily on a bat, supervised the game from positions dangerously close to the wickets, and well on the field of play sat the two scorers, notching the runs on a piece of wood with a knife, and making a deeper cut every tenth run. As scoring was at a very slow rate, this method was quite sufficient, but no separate record of each man's total could be kept.

Although this was the general plan of the game in the early eighteenth century, there were still wide variations from district to district: shape and size of bat and wickets, number in the team, and a host of other details differed from village to village.

In 1774, after one of the matches between Kent and All England, it was decided that there must be some uniformity, and so a set of rules were drawn up for the game. By these, the two stumps had to be twenty-two inches high and six inches apart, the pitch twenty-two yards long and a scratch (crease) one inch wide made forty-six inches in front of the wicket.

At this time the team winning the toss not only could elect whether or not to bat, but also choose the pitch within a radius of thirty yards from a point fixed by the opposing team. The bowlers of the winning team immediately began a frantic search for slopes, hummocks, ditches, or other irregularities in the ground which suited their particular delivery.

Between 1744 and 1770 Kent and Surrey fought often for the championship, but by the latter date the supremacy in the field had passed to the most famous club perhaps of all time—the Hambledon Club, in Hampshire. The famous names—Nyren, Sueter, Powlett, Small, Harris, Brett, and the rest, blacksmiths, squires, butchers, and noblemen—raised the crude game to a science. On their immortal ground at Broad Halfpenny Down they developed slinging bowling and the modern straight bat which was made essential by the ball which no longer crept along the ground. There, on the springy grass of the down, and perhaps in the Bat and Ball Inn which stood close by, Cricket, if not born, certainly grew to manhood.

The rules did change, when circumstances forced them, as in 1774 when a certain Mr White of Reigate took his guard with a bat wider than the wicket. Immediately the 4¼-inch bat was decreed. Again, in 1777, because of the sharp quarrels which arose whether the ball had passed between the two stumps or not, it was decreed that a third should be added in the middle.

But brightly though the Hambledon star shone, an even more brilliant sun was looming over the horizon when in 1788, at Mr Thomas Lord's cricket-ground in London, the Marylebone Cricket Club was formed. Gradually control of the game, which for twenty years had rested in the wilds of Hampshire, passed to the capital, and in 1791, the old club had disappeared as an active body, its members dispersed throughout the country, carrying with them the gospel of Cricket. By the end of the century the game had become an essential part of the English summer, and a few of the public schools had already issued challenges although it was to be another twenty-five years before the fixtures became regular.

I

One feature of eighteenth-century Cricket which has disappeared—
for the good of the game—is betting. Matches were always played for
'something'—a piece of beef in local village matches, ten pounds a man
in bigger games, and sometimes one thousand guineas a side in a really
large contest. But this was to be expected in a country where gambling
was second only to eating and drinking as a national hobby.

Men bet on almost anything: Horse-racing, Cockfighting, Dog-
fighting, Dicing, and Card-playing were always present, of course, but
every opportunity was made to seek new diversions with an element of
chance. In the wealthy clubs thousands of pounds, and in the humble
inns hard-won shillings, would change hands on the result of two rain-
drops coursing down a windowpane, the day's weather, or the colour
of the coat of the next man to enter the room. Bets were made on most
outrageous contests, as, for example, when Lord Rockingham bet £5000
that he would drive five geese from Norwich to London more quickly
than Lord Orford would drive five turkeys over the same distance.
Another nobleman wagered the same amount that he could get sheep
sheared, the wool spun and woven into cloth, and the cloth made into
a suit between sunrise and sunset on the same day—and he won his bet
with a few minutes to spare.

Vast sums were won and lost at the cardtable where Loo, Quadrille,
and Whist were the favourite games of every class. Losses of the order of
£15,000 on an evening's game were not uncommon at the more exclusive
clubs patronized by the young sons of wealthy families, and once Lord
Stavordale, still under twenty-one, lost £11,000, then won it all back
on a single hand.

While gambling took place in every home except those of very strict
religious outlook, and in every inn, the really high stakes were to be
found in the clubs which sprang up like mushrooms in London and the
larger cities. The coffee-houses, begun in the middle of the seventeenth
century, had an amazing popularity, and before many years a number of
them began to attract one particular type of customer—the writers
would meet at one, the Horse-racing enthusiasts at another, the actors
at a third, and so on. Here men could meet others with the same interests,
and the coffee-house keepers soon saw the advantage of keeping their
regular customers satisfied by reserving a separate room for them. From
this beginning some houses began providing meals and wines for the
'inner circle,' and later even bedrooms. Some were so successful that

A cockpit

the public coffee trade was closed, and the premises became exclusively clubs for members: White's, Brook's, and Boodle's, three of the most famous, are still in existence to-day.

But for those who could not obtain admission to the very exclusive and fashionable clubs, nor afford the extravagant ways of living expected of members, there were hundreds of simple, humble gatherings in almost every town in the country. Men of similar interests—Angling, Cricket, Boxing, Farming, and a host of others, would meet once a week or month in the private rooms of an inn for an early dinner, a long cheerful evening with plenty of drink, and finally a late supper. The conversation, we are told by a French diarist, usually started correctly, but soon wandered off to horses, hunting, and even less reputable subjects.

Numerous though the clubs were, they interested only a minute fraction of the thousands that poured into the ever-swelling, ever-bursting cities. The factories and city life took all of the new arrivals' energy and most of their time: the fields in which once they had played were every year being pushed farther and farther away as rows of dingy houses crawled outward from the centre. It is little wonder, then, that the mass of working-people turned to the nearest and easiest amusements that offered themselves. The problem, still acute to-day, of vast crowds willing to pay to be passively entertained, rather than to seek active amusements, had begun in earnest.

Unfortunately, the nearest, easiest, and cheapest amusement available, particularly to the slum-dwellers, was drink. Spirits, especially gin, were ridiculously cheap, and inns advertised proudly, "Drunk for a penny, dead drunk for twopence"—and they were by no means exaggerating. Drunken men, women, and children, together with those blinded as a result of drinking the raw spirit, were one of the commonest sights in the streets of London and the large cities, until the Government, in 1736, imposed a heavy tax on spirits which drove the townsfolk to the less dangerous beer and the completely harmless tea.

Cockfighting too enjoyed an immense popularity with all classes of men, the earl and the beggar rubbing shoulders in the noisy, hot, jostling cockpits to watch the vicious game birds battle to the death. Here too gambling added even more wickedness to the proceedings, and those who could not, or would not, pay their debts were hoisted to the ceiling of the pit in a basket rather like the car of a balloon.

As well as challenge-matches between individual owners, there were

The prize ring

inter-village, inter-town, and even county cockfights. For weeks before-hand the birds would be fed on special secret diets, often containing the most revolting ingredients, to give them courage and fire, and on the day of the main beaks, claws, and spurs would be delicately filed and sharpened to make them more deadly.

Bear- and Bull-baiting still had a strong following, though both were often conducted with more kindness than in the past. They were still cruel, but the bull frequently wore a muzzle over its nose and mouth, the most tender parts, to protect them from the dogs. In return the hounds had a better chance of survival because the bull's horns were often tipped with blunt caps. Sometimes dogs were allowed to jump at captive bears at a shilling a time, and a prize of ten shillings was given to the owner of the dog that leaped the highest. Despite the change for the better, however, there were still hundreds of the poor animals, covered with old scars and half-healed wounds, dragged round the country at the end of chains for baiting in the old fashion.

Among the lower elements of the mob there was no pastime half as enjoyable and exciting as a good public execution, and as there were over two hundred crimes for which a person could be sentenced to death, there was no shortage of entertainment.

Hours before the time appointed the square would be thronged with the joking, smoking, chewing crowd, while windows overlooking the scaffold were packed with spectators who had paid high prices for their seats. (For more fashionable or more notorious criminals grandstands were even erected.) It was this type of person who, when sport in his own line was rather quiet, paid his penny admission to Bethlehem Hospital (Bedlam, the lunatic asylum) to tease the unfortunate inmates.

But all was not quite as black as this, and a little way up the scale of decency could be found the boxing-booths. In the earlier years of the century it is true the fights were little better than the blood battles in the cockpits and bullrings, but before 1799 Boxing had acquired the first glimmerings of respectability.

The schools of Duelling, Cudgel-play, and Swordsmanship often taught Boxing as a side-line, and this gradually became their main business as the carrying of weapons fell out of fashion. In addition to instruction in the use of the fists, the 'Academies' put on fighting-matches —savage contests often resulting in injury, blindness, or even death. The pugilists showed animal courage and ferocity but little skill, the pair standing in the centre of the roped-in enclosure, battering each other into bloodstained insensibility. Various men set themselves up as 'Champions of England,' but Boxing appealed only to the coarsest of men until Jack Broughton, from his amphitheatre near Tottenham Court Road, reorganized the sport.

Broughton, like all other successful prize-fighters of the day, was 'adopted' by a wealthy nobleman, in this case the Duke of Cumberland. His arena was very popular with those who liked this type of entertainment, and to prevent disappointed supporters entering the enclosure to give assistance to their 'man' when he appeared to be having the worst of the battle, he raised the stage six feet from the floor as it is to-day.

The famous Broughton rules which had such a great effect in raising the standard of Boxing were issued in 1743. By these a square a yard in each direction was chalked in the centre of the ring, and at the beginning of each round—that is, after each fall, for a round went on until one man was on the ground—the two contestants had to toe opposite sides. If a boxer failed to get back into position within thirty seconds of being knocked down he was considered beaten. This meant of course that there were no intervals. The rules also stated that only the fighters, their seconds, and Mr Broughton himself were allowed on the stage during a contest, and also insisted on such elementary details as prohibiting a boxer from seizing his opponent by the legs or breeches or hitting him when he was on his knees.

Although Broughton used mufflers, a crude form of glove, for instruction and training-bouts, they were considered too 'soft' for real matches, and the bare-fisted bruisers, their hands pickled in strong soda to make them leathery and hard, battered, kicked, and bit their way through round after round until one of them was senseless or too badly mauled to continue.

For those who preferred their entertainment not to be spattered with blood, either human or animal, there was an ever-widening choice as the century progressed. The annual fair, for example, remained a great event in the lives of every one, though as the century progressed the little serious buying and selling which remained from the old days began to dwindle. Fairs were for fun, and though the world was becoming rapidly more sophisticated and knowledgeable, the crowds then, as now, gladly paid to be tricked by the old fakes that had duped their medieval ancestors. The toy- and trinket-stalls, the eating-houses, the ropewalkers, the conjurers, contortionists, wrestlers, and musicians of earlier days still claimed full houses, but new entertainments were creeping in. The waxworks showing such displays as "The Court of France" drew gasps

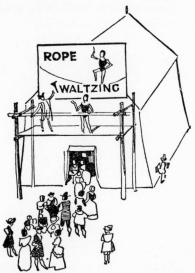

"... *the ropewalkers, the conjurers, contortionists, wrestlers ...*"

of amazement from the countryman and his wife who then turned to goggle (for a penny) into the hole of a peepshow. Here he could see "The Siege of Gibraltar" or other famous military exploits in three dimensions and colour, or else pictures of a firework display in which

The peepshow

light shining through pinholes in the paper made a most effective sight. Sometimes outlandish animals such as camels were put on show, and even, occasionally, miniature menageries made an appearance.

Punch too had begun his two-centuries-long career which shows no sign of waning in popularity, and the real theatre moved its companies *en bloc* to the tents and booths of the fairground. For sixpence one could see the most famous actors of the day in anything from the ancient moralities to Shakespeare, and though the price of admission to the shows was rather high in relation to the wages of the day, one got value for money. One company at Bartholomew Fair gave *The True and Ancient History of Maudlin the Merchant's Daughter of Bristol*, a variety of singing and dancing acts, and a harlequinade all on the same programme.

"*. . . roundabouts and Big Wheels offered a new thrill . . .*"

While the seeds of all of these entertainments had been present in the Tudor fair, even if not fully developed, mechanical entertainment belonged to the eighteenth century. Swingboats, almost identical with our own, and crude roundabouts and Big Wheels offered a new thrill to those whose senses had been deadened and still had money burning a hole in their pockets. The clumsy wooden merry-go-round, or whirligig, creaked round and round, and the Up and Down trundled over and over, powered by the proprietors who must have earned their money in a very hard way.

The more sedate and the family groups for whom the fairs were perhaps too expensive found the many pleasure-gardens in London a steady, popular attraction. These small enclosed parks which were such a feature of the eighteenth-century capital clustered thickly round the fringe of the city—Spring Gardens, Marylebone Gardens, Sadler's Wells, Islington Spa, Bagnigge Wells, Ranelagh Gardens, and, most famous of all, Vauxhall Gardens.

The resorts differed, naturally, but in most, for a few pence admission, one could wander along the laid-out walks, through ornamental arches, and past miniature lakes, or, lying in the shade of the trees, listen to popular light music from the central pavilion. Most provided refreshments in the shape of teas and cake, but some offered chicken-and-ham suppers in shady glades and alcoves. Ranelagh Gardens, the favourite of the upper classes, had an enormous rotunda, or dome, where fashionable ladies and dandies walked to show off their clothes, or sipped tea in one of the boxes that mounted up in tiers. Some gardens—Marylebone was one of the chief—specialized in firework displays; others had a ring, rather like that in a modern circus, where horses gave shows, and towards the end of the century a few offered astounded spectators the thrill of aviators making balloon-ascents.

Apart from the fireworks and an occasional illuminated balloon-flight, most of the gardens' attractions were for the sunny days and soft warm evenings of summer. When the autumn returned, with bad weather and darkness, the gates were closed, and many of the patrons turned to the comfort of the theatres which, as the century progressed, appealed to a much wider audience than the Court circle which had been their chief support during the Stuart period. The strict Puritan influence which had so severely frowned on acting and playgoing was rapidly weakening, and the middle classes in particular flocked to the performances.

There were many brilliant actors, headed by David Garrick and Mrs Siddons. These two in particular waged a campaign against wealthy patrons who still continued to sit on the stage, and after a struggle managed to get them banished to their rightful place in the body of the theatre. There were minor improvements in the stage and its lighting too, and plays tended more and more to be acted in historical costume rather than in the ordinary dress of the day, though this was by no means general.

Unfortunately, the art of playwriting entered a hundred-year period of depression, and apart from the three famous comedies, *The School for Scandal*, *The Rivals*, and *She Stoops to Conquer*, few of the many dramatic pieces written and produced in the eighteenth century are seen or even read to-day by the general public. The actors fell back on the inevitable Shakespeare and other established pieces, helped out by short one-act 'entertainments' before the main play.

What the eighteenth-century dramatists lacked in imagination and skill, however, they tried to make up for in elaboration and machinery. In one play, the story of Orpheus and Eurydice, the opening scene represented a dunghill in front of a farmhouse. A small egg on the heap grew bigger and bigger in front of the audience's eyes until it cracked, and out stepped a boy Harlequin. Later in the play, as Orpheus played his lute, 'shoots' appeared from 'rocks' on the stage. These grew into 'trees,' 'flowered,' dropped their 'petals,' and finally 'fruited.' The audience, middle-class citizens and no longer the sophisticated Court, loved every moment, and clamoured for more and more of the extravagant spectacles of colour and wonder.

When the theatres closed for the summer months the famous composer Handel took over one of them, the Haymarket, for a season of opera, a fairly new entertainment. Throughout the winter he toured the Continent to find the finest singers and musicians for his works, most of which were on religious themes. When a few years later Handel fell into disfavour because of political troubles Italian grand opera became the rage of the fashionable circle, and even English works such as *The Beggar's Opera*, which was based on popular tunes of the day and folk-songs, enjoyed a period of vogue. Yet opera, English or Italian, religious or secular, appealed to only a limited number of people even if one includes those who had no love of music but went because it was the correct thing to do. A great many people too, who might have gone, were away from the city during Mr Handel's performances, for among those who could afford it the new pastime of holidaying at the spas was becoming increasingly popular.

Begun originally as medical resorts in the seventeenth century, the spas had an amazing increase both in number and size during the reigns of the first two Georges. London itself was ringed with them: Dulwich, Streatham, Islington, Richmond, and many others boasted healing waters, gaming-rooms, and general entertainments on a modest scale.

To these near-by resorts the ordinary citizens of London poured at week-ends and in the evenings; the more wealthy—tradesmen, merchants, and the like—went a little farther afield to the more exclusive Epsom Spa, while those with more money and leisure than they knew how to use travelled to distant Bath, Scarborough, or Tunbridge Wells.

As the century progressed, more and more towns 'discovered' healing springs, and, seizing their opportunity, quickly built baths, pump-rooms, assembly rooms, tea-rooms, theatres, bookshops, parks, and promenades to cater for the few genuine invalids and swarms of pleasure-seekers that descended upon them. Mothers took their daughters to find husbands; penniless noblemen searched for wealthy heiresses to marry; young politicians and clergymen seeking promotion followed in the trains of lords and bishops. Beneath these seekers flocked lesser seekers, and smooth-tongued tricksters preyed on all.

At the larger spas a master of ceremonies was appointed to regulate the social life of the towns and to organize fashion. Some, like Beau Nash, were virtually little kings whose word was law, but they did do some permanent good by insisting on improved roads, houses, and street-lighting in their own tiny kingdoms.

Although each master of ceremonies drew up his own rules, life in all of the spas ran much the same course. A dip in the hot baths about nine began the day, and was followed by an hour in the coffee-house with the newspaper. Breakfast at ten was a public affair, often the occasion for a party. The morning was rounded off with a visit to church, not because of any sincere religious beliefs, but because it offered an opportunity to show off one's clothes and to gossip.

The afternoon until dinner at three was spent riding, walking, shopping, or browsing in bookshops. Polite visits and more gossip, broken by the latest craze for afternoon-tea, passed the time until the evening entertainment at the theatre, ballroom, or gambling-house. With a heavy supper between ten o'clock and midnight, dancing, cards, and wine kept the spa amused until the early hours of the morning when the sedan-chairs bore the tired and often intoxicated revellers to their lodgings.

So the dandies preened and strutted, and for a short while the spas held undisputed sway, but by mid-century there had risen in the sky of pastimes a new star that was to continue growing in brilliance right up to the present day. As a century earlier doctors had discovered the value of certain fresh-water springs, so other medical men now put forward the idea that sea-water had even greater health-giving properties. Before this date the sea had been considered only as an inconvenient but necessary method of travel, a source of fish, and a means of bringing foreign luxuries to England. Now, drunk or bathed in, it was supposed to cure all diseases.

One by one the pleasure-seeking wealthy families sampled the seaside, and quite suddenly tiny, poverty-stricken fishing-hamlets became famous, particularly those within easy coaching distance of London, for the crowded city was always ready to try new amusements. Brighton, then Brighthelmstone, became the most fashionable almost at once, though Margate and Ramsgate, which could be reached fairly quickly by sea, drew crowds of those who could spare only a week-end. With inland spa and seaside resort in open competition, Horace Walpole said contemptuously, "One would think the English were ducks—they are ever waddling off to water."

For a while—that is, before they realized their good fortune—the seaside villages offered accommodation which was very cheap compared with the spas, but soon, as assembly halls were built and entertainments given in imitation of the inland towns, prices rose from a few shillings a week for a cottage to as many guineas.

Despite the prices, however, the rush to the coast increased, for the new resorts could offer all that the inland spas did, and much more besides. There were the views of the sea and cliffs, the pure air, the beaches and the bathing, and when in addition to the Prince Regent's adoption of Brighton the royal family spent the summer at other coastal villages, the seal of popularity was finally affixed. It must be realized, though, that holidays were still the privilege of the upper classes: the ordinary workman did not have any period away from work long enough to enable him to travel to the coast by the slow horse transport even if he could have afforded it.

By the middle of the century bathing-machines had been installed at a few of the tiny towns, and by the end they had become the very symbol of the seaside. These 'machines' were small wooden cabins on very high wheels with steps leading down from a door in the front. The bather entered the machine which, while he was removing his clothes, was dragged into the sea by a horse so that the steps pointed away from the shore. When the water was well above the axles the horse was uncoupled and taken ashore as the bather opened his door to surrender himself into the sadistic arms of the "dipper."

These creatures—for so most of those who met them would have described them—were usually ex-fishermen or their wives who, standing waist-deep in the water all day, ruled their tiny patch of sea with a rod of iron. Immediately the shivering bather appeared he was seized by the dipper, and plunged under the waves—for his health, of course. Pleas, cries, entreaties, and clinging on to the machine doorway were equally useless: in the dipper's clutches you received the double-sea-water treatment, externally by submersion and internally by the glasses of water the monster forced you to drink. If the bather went too far for his safety it was the leathery-voiced dipper—man or woman—who ordered him back, and even the formidable Prince Regent himself obeyed his dipper as meekly as a lamb.

As every one went into the sea naked there was no mixed bathing. At some resorts there were fixed hours for men's and women's dips and at others the sexes were kept to opposite ends of the beach. A few towns, fortunate enough to have a number of coves, solved the difficulty by having a ladies' beach and a gentlemen's.

Although a surprising number remained at the seaside through the winter, dipping daily in the icy water, the majority returned to the city, with the falling leaves. The towns re-awakened from their summer sleep, and the endless round of concerts, balls, prize-fights, card-parties, eating, and drinking kept the grown-ups fully amused. For children no longer able to play long hours out of doors winter had always been a dull season unless the large families could agree to play the old indoor ring games, but in the eighteenth century the tiny trickle of toys began to grow into a steady rivulet, swelling yearly until it reached the tidal wave of the twentieth century.

A sign of the times was that tradesmen were beginning to devote their whole business to catering for children, for as early as 1738 Martin's Toy and Cap Shop at the Sign of the Three Rabbits, in London, was advertising for sale dressed babies (dolls), wax and naked babies. The tiny figures became cheaper and more plentiful, and it is possibly because of this that the name changed from 'baby' to 'doll' (short for Dorothy), though no one knows exactly when or why.

The beautiful and expensive dolls' houses continued to be imported from Germany and Holland for adult collectors and the wealthiest children, and even our own famous designers, the Adam Brothers and Chippendale, did not think it beneath their dignity to make exquisite miniatures for their noble customers. But new, simpler toy homes were appearing in the shops, obviously intended for children's use alone. Their strong, plain design and cruder, sturdier equipment made them much more suitable for the rough-and-tumble of play, and opened a new

Seaside holiday

delightful world, if not to the poorer children at least to those of the middle class.

Girls are easily, if expensively, satisfied, dolls and their accessories answering most of the feminine needs, but boys demand a much wider range of toys to keep them amused. In the seventeen-hundreds a beginning was made in satisfying this desire.

There were countless armies of flat tin and lead soldiers in the shops, for with the struggles in India, Canada, and America war was in every one's mind. For less aggressive moods there were model windmills—most unrealistic and terribly dull—and wooden pull-along coaches-and-four. These were all traditional toys, and the Age of Reason was capable of much better when the discoveries of science began to filter through even to the nursery. While it seemed still a miracle that men could float upward in the newly invented balloon, the toymen brought out miniatures which, complete with tiny gondola, drifted towards the ceiling on the end of a piece of string. But even more exciting was the magic lantern, an offering to children by the science that had created the telescope and microscope a little earlier. Powered by one or two candles, the image of the hand-painted slides on the whitewashed wall was flickering and patchy, but even so it must have meant much more to the Hanoverian children with their limited range of amusements than the most elaborate television-set does to a child to-day.

In the middle of the century table games suddenly burst into a blaze of popularity. For 150 years after its first introduction to England the Game of Goose had made little progress, but in the 1750's the original game and a number of variations began to stream from the printing-presses. Most stuck very closely to the rules of Goose, altering only the forfeits and rewards and the actual pictures in the squares. In the Royall Passtyme of Cupid, for example, the winner found himself, after romantic setbacks, in square 63, the Garden of Love. The goal of other games was a castle, but the Game of Human Life, while adhering to the principles of Goose, struck a novel and serious note:

The path in this case consisted of eighty-four squares, each representing one year of life, and ranging from 1, the Infant, to 84, the Immortal Man. The rules of the game advised the use of a six-sided Teetotum as the introduction of dice into moral homes might lead to dreadful wickedness, but whatever the means, the players worked their way through squares 1–12 (Infancy and Youth), 13–24 (Manhood),

25–36 (Prime of Life), 37–48 (Sedate Middle Age), 49–60 (Old Age) 61–72 (Decrepitude), and 73–84 (Dotage). It was a most uplifting game, the whole of life's journey being liberally strewn with good advice and punishments for those who sinned.

The belief, which was to grow so strong in Queen Victoria's reign, that children's games should educate as well as amuse, got off to a very firm start at the end of the eighteenth century with a flood of historical and geographical pastimes, based usually on the race or Goose idea. The Royal Genealogical Pastime made little attempt to coat its pill for it consisted of a series of squares, each bearing the name and date of a monarch, and as the unfortunate child moved his counter along he was expected to memorize these facts together with a short biography of that particular sovereign on the reverse of the board.

A Journey through Europe, typical of many board games of the period, was much more attractive. Starting at York (1), the player moved his counter across a numbered map of Europe, the tour going through Berwick (2), Edinburgh (3), Iceland, Scandinavia, Russia, Poland, the Mediterranean countries, and ending in London (77). At the halts one was expected to learn such snippets of information as "No. 39, Smyrna. He who rests here must wait two turns to load a ship with raisins for England," or "He who rests at No. 50, Sicily, must stay one turn to visit the famous burning Mount Etna."

In the dying years of the century jigsaw puzzles appeared on the market, but, as fretsaws had not been invented, the wood was cut with a jeweller's saw which will not turn very easily. The resultant pieces were consequently almost straight-sided, or at best slightly wavy, and completely unlike the modern interlocking variety. Like the race games, jigsaws were largely instructional, the finished pictures being of geographical, historical, or Scriptural subjects, but as the pieces were so large and few in number they were suitable only for smaller children.

Perhaps the most important of all in the history of children's pastimes during the period was the appearance in 1744 of a small book by John Newberry entitled:

A Little Pretty Pocket Book intended for the Instruction and Amusement of Little Master Tommy and Pretty Miss Polly with an agreeable letter to be read from Jack the Giant Killer, also a ball and a pincushion the use of which will infallibly make Tommy a good Boy and Polly a good Girl.

K

There had been a number of books for children before this, but they had been heavy, serious volumes of instruction in religious matters, behaviour, Latin, or other school subjects: the "Pretty Pocket Book," although it put 'Instruction' first in its title, made 'Amusement' its main aim, and so can claim the credit for being the first real book for boys and girls to enjoy.

Its success was immediate, and other booksellers began to cater for the new readers, though it must be remembered that a large proportion of the population still could not read or write. Fables, traditional tales, and nursery rhymes were widely sold, often by pedlars in the form of chapbooks—badly printed, crudely illustrated pamphlets—for a penny or a halfpenny. There were not many original stories written for children at the time, a large amount of material being translated from the French, and it is surprising to learn that most fairy stories which we regard as so essentially English—Cinderella, Sleeping Beauty, Red Riding Hood, Puss in Boots, and Bluebeard—arrived in British nurseries from abroad.

Though we may smile at, or perhaps pity, the simple amusements of eighteenth-century children, they represented a great advance on those of a hundred years earlier. Toyshops and books alike declared that the existence of boys and girls as beings in their own right had been recognized at last. The next century, despite the horrors of the infant slavery in factory, mine, and chimney, was to see complete victory.

CHAPTER VII

The Nineteenth Century

AS England slipped into the nineteenth century the great Industrial Revolution was well on its way to completion. Great factories poured out a never-ending stream of goods for the whole world, and in return undreamed-of wealth rolled into Britain. Every day saw a new invention which brought in its train a string of discoveries; the discoveries in their turn lead to yet more invention. The steam-engine had taken the romance—and, more important, the discomfort, uncertainty, and expense—from travel by land and sea; big new boarding-schools blossomed overnight to cater for the sons of the new wealthy class, and boys from the ends of the kingdom were brought together to beat out a new way of life; the telegraph, the penny post, and the newspaper spread information, news, and ideas more widely than anyone would have dreamed a few years earlier. The speed of life, it seemed, was coupled to the whirring wheels of the steam-engine, going faster and ever faster.

The machine was the King of the Victorian Age: it brought the millowner his fortune and power and the workmen his wages. It offered the artisan the chance to rise in wealth and position. Man's muscles, it would seem, were fast becoming obsolete.

Yet, though the machine dominated so much of Victorian life, it did not enter directly into the field of recreation until the latter years of the century, and as a reaction to things mechanical in working hours, there was an unparalleled outburst of interest in active sports and games in leisure time. Men and women, cooped up in the great cities and shackled to a clanking engine for six days a week, fifty-two weeks a year, craved to use their bodies in some free activity. The cruel old sports that had entertained their fathers and grandfathers were fading in the kindlier atmosphere that was abroad. Animal-baiting, for example, had almost disappeared by 1835, when it was legally banned. Public cockfights were suppressed in 1849, but even by then the sport was tending to become localized in its popularity. Dog-fighting, though not abolished by law, had lost favour in the public eye. A vacuum existed in the lives of millions of working-people which could have been filled with revolutionary political ideas as it was in so many European countries, but fortunately for England a lead came from the schools and universities at just the right moment. Britain surrendered itself to sport.

At the beginning of the century the only team game that was organized on a large scale was Cricket, but by the time it closed almost all of our present-day sports were in full cry. Old games were brought up to date with proper rules, games were introduced from the ends of the Empire, and when these ran short new games were invented.

In common with the other savage sports, the traditional mass football game was rapidly disappearing at the beginning of the nineteenth century, and was kept alive mainly in the public schools, each of which had its own rules. City schools with their tiny cobbled courts obviously could not play the same game as those in the country with acres of fields. At Rugby, for example, Football was still a wild chase with up to three hundred players in which kicking played a major part, but a player blocked by a mob of opponents could catch the ball in his arms and run with it towards his own goal until he was free to kick forward again. The attackers meanwhile were not allowed to advance beyond the spot where the ball had been caught until the player had punted it himself or had placed it for another of his own side to kick. These were the rules until the famous day in 1823 when William Ellis, clasping the ball to his body, ran towards the enemy goal, and by so doing sowed the seeds of modern Rugby, though much development had still to take place before our twentieth-century game evolved.

The idea of carrying the ball took hold, and was copied by other schools so that soon there was bitter rivalry between the Dribblers of the old style, who believed that the ball should be kicked, and the Handlers. Apart from the main ideas, however, there was little agreement between the many supporters of each style—rules and numbers in a team varying from school to school. By the middle of the century, however, with adjustments here and agreements there, the main outlines of our modern games were present, although in Soccer, among other odd practices, there were still eight forwards.

In 1863 an attempt was made to join the dribblers and the handlers into one composite game, but when negotiations broke down the break was final, the Soccer followers forming the Football Association in 1863 and their rivals the Rugby Football Union eight years later.

The new organized Football as opposed to the mad rough-and-tumble was the answer that half of England had been longing for: teams burst into life up and down the land, representing town, village, factory, school, or army unit, and when in 1867 the ban in Soccer on passing the ball forward—a rule which forced a man to dribble through on his own and so prevented team play—was lifted, the game received an impetus which set the seal on its wild popularity. So many teams battled every week that in 1872 the Football Association organized a knockout competition for a challenge cup as a reward.

It does seem unfortunate that an age which took part in sport to a degree never equalled before or since should have coincided with an age when dress was at its stuffiest and heaviest. Football was one of the more sensibly dressed games, but even so the players charged up and down the field in the mud with long knickerbockers tied below the knee, long stockings, striped shirts, and sometimes caps. They wore their everyday boots or shoes with sometimes a few bars of leather nailed across the soles for grip, and not until the 1880's was special footwear with hardened toe-caps and studs available.

In the eighties too a far more sinister introduction was made in Soccer—the professional player. Until about 1885 every one had been an amateur, playing Football solely for the love of the game, but now came men who played as a job. Not that professional sport is necessarily a bad thing, but it does create a tendency among so many people merely to watch the experts rather than take part themselves. For good or ill, however, in 1888 the teams of all professional players formed the Football League, and, taking over the old challenge cup of the F.A., founded the amazingly successful series of Cup Tie matches.

Though real Football had not been born in 1800 Cricket entered the nineteenth century, if not fully grown, a well set-up youth. In the South of England, at least, many of the modern practices were followed, though occasional freakish games, such as the one played on horseback, showed that cricket was not quite adult yet. In the North the game had developed rather more slowly, and when Nottinghamshire played an All-England eleven in 1817 they were allowed to field twenty-two men.

Heavy betting on the result of matches connected Cricket closely with its origins in the eighteenth century, and like the top-hat and bow-ties as cricketing wear, did not finally disappear until after 1850. In the first part of the century the batsmen, whose equipment and technique had developed rapidly, were completely on top of the bowlers, who were hampered by the rule which forbade the arm to be raised above shoulder-level when delivering a ball. Consequently the batsmen hit the relatively simple bowling for terrific scores, and no doubt many of them were disappointed to see the modern style of delivery made legal by the M.C.C., in 1864. From that date onward things were much more evenly matched, though the following year saw the first appearance of the man who broke many a bowler's heart, however he bowled—W. G. Grace.

The gigantic and legendary Dr Grace, perhaps the most famous cricketer of all time, absolutely dominated the 1870's, a decade which ranks very important in the history of the game, for in 1873 the county championship was first fought, and in 1878 the Australians made their first tour, beating the M.C.C. in one day.

Cricket had very early accepted the professional player into its ranks, the first Gentlemen (amateurs) versus Players (professionals) match being played in 1806. The paid full-time players, however, formed only a nucleus of each team, the majority still being those who played in their spare time. This situation was maintained throughout the century, and indeed until recent times, so that Cricket has been able to avoid many of the problems that attend such fully professional sports as League Football.

Rowing is often regarded as a traditional English sport, but though a few schools in the eighteenth century took it up, it was considered a somewhat uncouth pastime, suitable only for youths and the watermen, who, incidentally, had been holding an annual race since 1715. This contest was begun by the actor Thomas Doggett, to commemorate the accession of King George I, and, because of the prize, a scarlet tunic with a large silver badge on the arm, was, and still is, known as Doggett's Coat and Badge. By 1800, however, gentlemen, particularly those at university, began to look more favourably on Rowing, even though their boats were rather clumsy vessels with anything from four to ten oars. Soon after the turn of the century, too, London, as one might expect, began to take an interest, and three Rowing-clubs for amateurs were formed. Oxford and Cambridge, having only narrow rivers, were soon in difficulty as the sport increased in popularity, and in 1820 the bumping-races were introduced. After a few experimental years the boats were stationed at 100-yard intervals along the bank of the river, and all struck out at a pistol-shot, the object being to bump the boat immediately ahead. If this occurred the two boats withdrew, and in the next day's race changed places in the starting order, so that a good crew could eventually work up to the leading position.

Rowing eventually roused such interest that in 1829 Oxford challenged their rivals, Cambridge, to a race with eight-oared boats on the Thames. The match was purely a private one, and no one was more surprised than the universities when a vast crowd estimated at twenty thousand people appeared at Henley on the day of the race, which Oxford won. The next Boat Race, seven years later, attracted a similar crowd, and the Henley tradesmen and innkeepers, delighted at the wealth the crowds of spectators poured into their pockets, seized the chance to establish an annual regatta there independent of the University race.

The Oxford-Cambridge challenge was issued at intervals of a few years until 1856 when it became the famous annual event we know to-day, but its present course on the Thames from Putney to Mortlake was not fixed until 1862. What is rather remarkable is that from the very first event the Boat Race has fascinated millions of people who have no interest in, or connexion with, either university, yet fanatically adopt one or the other as 'theirs.'

Rowing was a reasonably inexpensive pastime for a group of enthusiasts who had the sea or a suitable river at hand, so that clubs sprang up all over the country, attracting good following, either for racing or merely leisurely paddling. But Sailing never made any attempt to appeal to any but the wealthy. Yachting was fashionable with a certain class of the aristocracy, but the clubs were exclusive, and went out of their way to make the sport more expensive by fixing a minimum size for boats— the Royal Yacht Club would accept nothing below twenty tons. Boats grew bigger and bigger, and the fact that the man with the longest purse could always build the fastest vessels tended to kill interest in yacht-racing. It was rather a blow to the Sailing experts—and the public too—when the United States schooner *America*, in 1851, showed a clean pair of heels to our best boats, and so won the cup which repeated attempts for over a century have failed to regain.

With the growth of interest in Rowing, and especially, as we shall see later, in the seaside, there was a rapid increase in the number who took up Swimming. It was no longer a case of a few people being able to swim through necessity, but of a large number swimming for sheer enjoyment. Liverpool, with great clear-sightedness, opened the first public swimming-bath in 1829, while London, whose river was at this time unspeakably filthy, had to its disgrace to wait for another twenty-one years for its first swimming-pool.

Like the baby who having mastered the skills of walking turns to the difficulties and joys of running and jumping, the new swimmers, in addition to extending their activities to racing and diving, invented Football in Water, or Aquatic Handball. This, like most games in their early days, was a rough-and-tumble scramble with few rules, and had teams ranging from three to fourteen in number. If played in a swimming-bath the ends formed the goals, the players touching the ball down as in Rugby, but when played in the open sea, as it often was, posts or buoys, as far apart as the players' wishes or swimming ability allowed, marked the limits. A favourite trick, we are told, was to hide the ball in the trunks, and to swim under water towards the enemy goal, but this and all other such delightful dodges were banished when the official Water Polo rules were drawn up in 1880.

Captain Webb's swim across the Channel in 1875, a feat which seemed as impossible then as crossing the North Sea in the water seems to us to-day, gave a terrific impetus to Swimming, and eleven years later the Amateur Swimming Association was formed to regulate the sport and its activities.

Akin to Swimming is Athletics, and although running races and leaping and throwing of weights of different kinds were traditional in the English countryside, they were haphazard and unorganized. Modern Athletics, like so many of our recreations, began in the universities and schools, and until the 1860's was almost exclusively a sport for the gentry who had been educated in them. A few school and university meetings were held in the first fifty years, but soon after the middle of the century Athletics began to break loose from its bonds when clubs of working-men, especially in the Midlands and North of England, were formed, despite considerable opposition from a section of the 'upper' classes who considered it poaching on their preserves. Throughout the sixties the movement, like a snowball, gathered size and popularity among the artisans of the cities, but unfortunately each club tended to go its own way. In 1880 the situation had become so impossible with clubs quarrelling and

Sporting dress

setting their own rules that twenty-seven of the larger groups decided to organize the Amateur Athletic Association to settle all disputes. From that moment Athletics really burst into life with clubs in every corner of the land.

Boundless energy seemed to fill the youth of the nineteenth century, and for those to whom Football, Cricket, Athletics, Rowing, or Swimming did not appeal as a means of disposing of their surplus vigour, less well-known and perhaps more exotic sports were introduced. Lacrosse from Canada and Polo from India had small but enthusiastic followings, while Hockey, a descendant of the savage Irish Hurling and the wild Scottish Shinty with a scrap of the brutal Welsh and English Bandy thrown in, drew larger numbers.

From the rough game of 1850 with its twenty-a-side teams, its unlimited pitch, its shoulder-charging and legalized hammering of shins with the stick to get possession of the hard rubber ball, Hockey gradually mellowed through the next thirty years. Rules were gradually added, overhauled, and amended so that by the end of the century, instead of the murderous brawl it had been fifty years earlier, Hockey was considered fit even for young ladies to play.

In the great enthusiasm for sport those whose sex, age, or shape made them unfitted for the hurly-burly of the games already mentioned were not forgotten. Gentler recreations were introduced or invented, several of them having the advantage that although they could be played quietly they could be stretched to give just as much exercise as one required. Foremost among these was Golf.

Although Blackheath Club had been founded in the first quarter of the century, Golf did not become at all popular in England until the last quarter. In Scotland, in the other hand, it was the national pastime, and improvements in the shape of better clubs with iron heads and balls of gutta-percha instead of feather-stuffed leather began to make themselves felt. When in 1888 the Royal and Ancient St Andrews Club drew up a list of rules, the English seemed to wake up to what they were missing, and golf-courses sprang up all over the country. When the royal family took up the game its popularity was settled beyond all doubt, and from that moment it has never looked back.

Less demanding on the body in general, though very good exercise for certain parts, was Archery, which enjoyed an immense vogue for much of the century. Like so many things which are discarded by the 'lower' classes as old-fashioned, and which are then taken up by the 'higher' classes, Archery, now no longer useful in war or hunting, was adopted as a sport, especially by ladies. Shooting, it seems, was of a very poor standard until in the fifties the experts analysed the techniques scientifically—and at once removed a great deal of the fun. In the last twenty years of the century the following dwindled until at the end only a relatively small group of enthusiasts remained. This rearguard has managed to keep the activity alive until our own day, when there has been a marked revival of interest.

For a meteoric rise to fame, there have been few movements to match Croquet in the nineteenth century. Introduced from France in 1852 where it had developed, possibly from the seventeenth-century game of Pell Mell, it became at once a craze, again especially among the ladies. Thirty years later the game had almost disappeared.

Although it appears so simple, Croquet was extremely complicated and difficult, and bore a marked resemblance to Billiards, for the player continued to play until he failed to score, when his opponent took over. Much of the skill lay in leaving the balls in a position that hindered the other side from scoring. To add to the similarity to Billiards, some players when confronted with a difficult shot lay on the ground to use the mallet-handle which was often tipped with rubber like a cue—a practice which was forbidden in 1897 when an unsuccessful attempt was made to bring the game back into popularity. Much Croquet, however, was of a far less serious type, as it afforded an ideal opportunity for young ladies and eligible bachelors to spend an hour or so in each other's company in pleasant surroundings and often free from the watchful eye of the elderly chaperon. In the end Croquet was killed by its own adopted child and rival, Lawn Tennis, and has unfortunately—for it was a game with many excellent points—now become rather a figure of fun.

'Real' Tennis, the indoor game which had been played since medieval times, was still an attraction in the nineteenth century, but it was still a sport of the wealthy. In an age when games of all sorts were booming it seemed a pity that such a good sport could not be simplified and brought within the reach of all classes of people, so in 1874 a Major Wingfield invented and patented a game called Sphairistike. This was played with pear-shaped, long-handled rackets similar to those used in 'real' Tennis, and small rubber balls on a grass court tapering from 30 feet in width at each end to 21 feet at its 4-foot net. Its success was immediate and almost bewildering, despite the fact that rules were made up by many players to suit themselves and their individual lawns. The court, however, soon developed into the rectangle we know to-day, and 'Lawn' Tennis had arrived.

In 1875 the game was introduced as a side attraction at the Croquet championships for light relief from the more serious and important entertainment, and few guessed then that within a very few years Lawn Tennis would have completely superseded the older game. Yet two years later, in 1877, the first All-England championships were held after a committee had decided on the rules of play and court-marking to be adopted. Even then the tiny crowd of two hundred keen followers present gave no hint of the phenomenal enthusiasm with which millions of players of all ages and classes would smash—or pat—the ball to and fro across the net in gardens and parks up and down the land within the next few years. Inexpensive, vigorous or gentle at will, and making fewer demands on strength than on skill, Lawn Tennis became, and has remained, the perfect 'mixed' game.

Great though the enthusiasm for competitive sports was, there were still those who liked their open-air exercise without the burning effort to beat the other fellow—or lady, for this field was, in many cases, open equally to both sexes. Riding, in one form or another, offered a perfect solution: the wealthy man and his family were in the saddles of their horses merely riding, or in pursuit of the fox, every moment that could be spared, and the poorer man, at least for the last twenty-five years of the century, raised a constant cloud of dust on the highway from the saddle of his bicycle in his far fewer leisure hours.

The horse, whether for a leisurely canter or for a full-blooded chase with the hounds, was still the supreme sport for those who had outgrown the wildness of the games field. A long hard day in the saddle pursuing the elusive fox, which had now virtually replaced the stag, was the height of most gentlemen's ambitions, and their greatest sorrow in life was the occasional hard frost which made Hunting impossible. The nobleman's life often centred on his horses whose status varied from a little above to a little below that of his wife and family. Professional men, tradesmen, and farmers all joined in the tail of the hunt, enjoying the actual ride perhaps less than the social standing which it was supposed to give them.

The bicycle, not having life and a personality, could not perhaps ever become as dear to the rider as his horse, but there is no doubt that

Sphairistike, or Lawn Tennis

the pleasure Cycling gave to millions was no less. Peculiar mechanical contraptions such as the hobby-horse had been in existence for many years, but they attracted little interest until the 'ordinary' bicycle, better known as the Penny-farthing, evolved in the 1860's. With its

The Penny-farthing

huge front wheel, often six feet in diameter, this fearsome and highly dangerous machine dominated the roads for twenty years, and established Cycling as a real pastime in England.

Perched high above the ground, the rider had a wonderful view of the road ahead—and he needed it for the deep potholes and large boulders which sprinkled the unmetalled roads of the day frequently hurled the intrepid cyclist over the handle-bars, head first to the ground. Cycling in the 'ordinary' days was without doubt a man's sport. It was the introduction of the Rover Safety cycle, in 1885, and of pneumatic tyres by Dr Dunlop three years later, that really made Cycling a universal pastime. The Rover Safety machine had two wheels almost the same size, and was driven by pedals and a chain in the modern manner. Ladies could, and did, take this bicycle to their hearts. A peculiar dress consisting of long baggy trousers, called Bloomers after the American lady who invented them, was adopted by thousands of young women as they swarmed in ever increasing numbers along the roads to join the men, some of whom still clung to the old-fashioned Penny-farthing as

The Rover Safety cycle

more manly equipment. Improvements which came out yearly—ball-bearings, better brakes, and, in 1894, the free-wheel, which overcame the difficulty of lifting one's feet from the pedals to a little bracket on the front of the frame when running quickly downhill, all helped to increase the huge army of 'bicyclists.'

Having captured the market of the more youthful, the cycle manu-facturers turned their attention to the more elderly who were afraid that they could never balance on two wheels. For these tricycles were made, sometimes single-seaters, but often double. Some had the two riders side by side, others one behind the other, while one machine sat the two back to back. The Excelsior One-Two-Three, in an effort to catch the eye, had each of its wheels a very different size. Other freak machines carried four, six, or even eight people at a time, but while the peculiar ones have disappeared, the ordinary bicycle still remains a firm favourite.

Sooner or later the season, the weather, or the darkness drove ball-player, hunter, and cyclist from field, forest, and highway, indoors to the most respected and loved of all Victorian institutions: Home. Here, with the large families that were normal in the nineteenth century, one need go no farther for entertainment. If the company was young Charades, Riddles, and Consequences were always popular, besides the toys that will be described later.

If the company was a little older Billiards was in a class by itself, for the modern Table Tennis and dartboard did not appear until the very last few years of the century, and apart from Battledore and Shuttlecock —a simple game in which a pair of players gently patted a shuttlecock to and fro with wooden bats—there was very little in the way of indoor 'sport.'

Billiards reached its present form quite early in the century, for after unsuccessful attempts to use an iron base for the table, the flat slate bed as is used to-day was adopted in 1827. Soon afterwards rubber cushions were first used, and about the same time the modern three-ball game replaced the older two- or four-ball ones.

In 1875 a young army officer in India suggested adding more coloured balls with different values to one of the 'pool' games played on a billiard-table, more or less as a joke, but his friends found the new pastime so enjoyable that it was retained. When they tried to find a name for it some one suggested that as they were all beginners at the new sport Snooker would be most fitting—in the army slang of the time a 'snooker' was a young cadet in his first year at the Royal Military Academy at Woolwich. The game itself was partly a joke and the name certainly one, but there was no doubt about its popularity, and even before the beginning of the twentieth century it was taking more and more men, particularly the younger ones, from the older Billiards.

But the green-baize tables have always had a masculine air about them so that neither Billiards nor Snooker was usually played when ladies were present. For mixed company in Victorian times Dancing was the fashionable entertainment, but as public balls were rather frowned upon, it was, in its more polite form, limited to those wealthy enough to own a large house and to be able to hire musicians.

Invitations were sent out well in advance, and each guest was provided with a card bearing a list of all the dances for the evening. Before the party really began the gentlemen moved round the room asking the ladies for the different dances, and entered their names against each item. Personal wishes entered little into the filling up of one's card as there were unwritten laws of conduct which compelled the gentleman to ask certain ladies for 'the pleasure,' and to dance more than twice with the same person was considered outrageously bad behaviour. A buffet of cold chicken, jellies, trifles, ices, and various wines was set out in an adjoining room, or, as the ballroom was usually on the first floor, downstairs. If a young lady's companion was an agreeable one and her next partner one she did not like she often suggested a visit to supper so that when the unpleasant one came to 'collect' her for 'his' dance she was either not to be seen or else in the middle of a large ice-cream, which had to be eaten very slowly.

To ensure that their children grew up naturally to the conventions of the formal balls, middle-class parents organized dances on exactly the same lines as the adults' for boys and girls from the age of about eight onward. While the little girls loved them from the start, there came a period in the lives of small boys when the buffet, with its lemonade, ices, and cakes, was much more attractive than the starched and frilled young ladies chattering in groups on the opposite side of the room.

For a change the adults were sometimes asked to wear fancy-dress, but formal, costume, or children's party, three dances dominated the ballroom—the waltz, the lancers, and the polka. Others came and went, but these three remained the favourites, and with the famous Strauss family to write so much of the music for them it was little wonder.

As the company grew older the favourite pastime of the middle and upper classes was the dinner-party and musical evening. Dinner itself was an occasion for very rigid rules of etiquette and procedure: perhaps some of the fun was in obeying the routine, but in any case the meal offered the hostess a wonderful opportunity of displaying the skill of her cook, her table, and her friends. Sometimes immediately after the last course the company separated, the gentlemen remaining in the dining-room to discuss business, sport, or politics over another glass of port and cigars while the ladies retired to the drawing-room to gossip about the children, fashions, and absent acquaintances.

L

When the party reunited the musical evening began: in the most wealthy houses famous musicians or even orchestras would play, but in the great majority the guests and hosts provided the entertainment. Every true Victorian of the middle class had his or her repertoire of ballads or comic songs, or piano or guitar solos, which would be given to the great delight of the performer, and, one supposes by the way the custom lasted, of the listeners as well.

In the 1870's a rival to the amateur singer was born, but as it took such a long time to find its real voice it did not prove a serious competitor until the attraction of the musical evening was beginning to fade. In 1877 the American Thomas Edison patented an office dictating-machine called the phonograph which used cylindrical records, first made of tinfoil, then later of wax. Eleven years later another American, Emile Berliner, searching for a 'voice' for his talking dolls, improved on the invention with his gramophone, which used flat disc records. But the idea was far too good for its original rather dull purposes, and by the eighties from the crude machines, turned at first by hand and then by clockwork, faint, scratchy, and metallic voices wheezed out songs and hymns from the depths of a tin horn. Though developments took place rapidly, the gramophone was not sufficiently perfect to provide good entertainment until the twentieth century, and remained largely an exciting novelty throughout our period.

There were evenings, of course, when there were no guests to dine, dance, or sing, or when the family was in no mood for the romping communal fun. There were too days when one wanted relief from games and companionship. Then the great Victorian custom of hobbies came into its own.

For girls and young ladies not yet caught up in the worries of household and servants there were always Sewing and Embroidery, which, besides being pleasant pastimes in themselves, fitted in well with the belief that recreation should be useful as well as enjoyable. With Embroidery the young lady could amuse herself, decorate all manner of household fabrics, and practise stitches that could be put to a far more practical purpose when she married.

Sketching and Watercolouring, also very popular with ladies in the summer months, had not quite such a definite use, but if one judges by the number of Victorian houses decorated with pictures painted by the mistress of the house before marriage, the time was not entirely wasted.

A musical evening

Collecting has always been an instinctive pastime, and in the nineteenth century with so much more being manufactured, there were many things to be treasured. For young ladies there were huge scrapbooks to be filled with pictures and cuttings from magazines; others with postcards and views sent by friends on holiday. Flowers gathered on summer rambles and picnics were pressed in the depths of heavy books and, browned and brittle, carefully pasted into notebooks during the dark winter evenings. If everything else in this line failed the young lady could fall back on re-arranging the sepia-coloured photographs in the family album.

The young gentlemen took their hobbies rather more seriously: some chased butterflies and beetles during the summer and spent the winter nights impaling and classifying their captives; others collected stamps, and when questioned on the educational value of their hobby had a ready answer in that it was of immense value to their study of geography.

Philately as a hobby began almost immediately after the introduction of stamps in 1840, and twenty-two years later had attracted such a following that the first British catalogue and the first monthly magazine on the subject were published. As more and more countries adopted the perforated adhesive stamp the hobby became more and more interesting so that by the end of the century collecting stamps was one of the phases through which almost every schoolboy, and many schoolgirls, passed. For many then, as now, Philately remained a life-long interest.

Photography too was largely a male recreation, possibly because the weight and size of much of the equipment in the early days demanded much more than a lady's strength. Invented almost simultaneously in France by Daguerre and in England by Fox Talbot, at the end of the 1830's, Photography was at first a very slow and cumbersome process, more suited to the scientific experimenter than to the ordinary person, especially as exposures often took an hour. For these early pictures the sitter often had to be clamped in an iron framework to prevent any movement during the agonizing minutes of exposure. One can quite understand why the majority of early photographs are of grim, determined, unsmiling victims.

As the plates in these first machines were put in the camera with the chemicals still wet, and had to be developed immediately the picture had been taken, the photographer had to take his dark-room with him.

Ingenious tentlike contraptions for this purpose were devised and added to the burden of boxes, chemicals, tripods, and general equipment that made Photography in its early days a hobby for the real enthusiast only.

But chemists and inventors worked hand in hand constantly to ease the lot of the picture-maker: plates became better and cameras lighter,

The amateur photographer

but it was not until the American, George Eastman, introduced the modern roll-film in 1888 that Photography became the push-button pastime we know to-day. Thousands scurried round the countryside with simple cameras costing only a few shillings 'snapping' whatever took their fancy, and then hurried home to develop their pictures in cellars, blacked-out kitchens, and sheds.

Photography is rather a half-way house between the theoretical hobbies such as collecting and the practical ones, and in an age so over-shadowed by the machine it was inevitable that mechanical modelling should be the pastime of many people. At night doctors and labourers, factory-hands and lawyers, men from the city and men from the farm, in sheds and workshops filed and hammered and operated whirring lathes. A steady stream of miniature steam-engines, railway locomotives, paddle- and screw-steamers, and other mechanical devices poured forth with painstaking labour and accuracy. For the younger, the less experienced, and those whose skill would never reach the precision required for the steam-driven models there was a flood of instructions for the making of magic lanterns, epidiascopes, electrical machines, fretwork and other wooden models, preferably those which 'did something' rather than just remained decorative.

Most of the hobbies, and, to a certain extent, the sports as well, demanded education. For full enjoyment all required the ability to read; Engineering needed mathematics and science; Coin-collecting was more interesting with a knowledge of history; while geography was important to get the fullest satisfaction from Stamp-collecting. Botany and biology lent greater pleasure to the flower-presser and to the insect-collector, and it may surprise many children to-day, who long for the hour when school will close behind them for ever, that one of the chief pastimes of the working-people for most of the nineteenth century was the search for learning.

Until 1870 schooling was not compulsory: a decent education was, except for a few isolated 'charity' schools and foundations, far beyond the means of most working parents. Men knew that knowledge was power, and that promotion at work often depended on their knowing more than the next man, but apart from the practical advantages there was a strong desire to learn, just for its own sake. As a result, evening classes at clubs and institutions were crowded to the doors with people eager to study; public libraries and reading-rooms which were springing up all over the country were full of men who having grasped the outlines of their subject were extending their knowledge further and further from books. Learned speakers travelled up and down the country giving public lectures which, though they might seem very dull to us, were followed earnestly and thoughtfully.

After 1870 every child had to attend school until he had reached a certain standard, so that long before the end of the century the vast majority of the population could both read and write.

The effect of this learning, together with the huge new steam-presses that made printing much cheaper and quicker, had a revolutionary effect on the leisure hours of the people of all classes. Millions of words aimed at all tastes and levels of society poured from the publishers every week; millions of hours which might have been spent in idleness (or, it must be admitted, perhaps engaged in some useful task) were spent with eyes glued to the printed page. There were magazines devoted to hobbies—Photography, Engineering, Stamps, Cycling, and later, Motoring. There were journals dealing with sports and outdoor recreations. Science, nature, geography, music, and art all had their periodicals. *Punch* lent a comic note, while illustrated weekly papers brought news in pictures and words from the corners of the earth. The upper classes had their publications which gave news of the aristocracy; the fashion magazines, aimed at the wealthy, appealed to every woman from the humblest scullery maid in the basement kitchen to the mistress in the drawing-room. The heavy, learned literary monthlies thundered out their criticisms for those who had the leisure to read them.

Scores and scores of booklets were written for the family containing recipes, household hints, and romantic stories for mothers, occasional practical or general articles for fathers, and pages for children. Women's papers appeared, and although many flourished and died in the space of a few years the sales rose higher and higher. Periodicals for children of all ages took a firm hold, but there was nothing quite like the all-picture comic papers of to-day. Daily papers were still serious, and did not have a wide appeal outside the more educated classes, but the Sunday newspapers whose standards were perhaps not so high, and which reported the less pleasant news items, were a wild success. Novels, often very lengthy, usually appeared in weekly parts before the issue of the complete book, and ranged from the immortal works of Dickens to the stupid romantic trash which formed such a large part of the reading diet of young servant-girls. Below even this, unfortunately, were the books, papers, and periodicals which enjoyed enormous sales, and which appealed to all that was coarse, beastly, and nasty in human nature. But high-brow or low-brow, seeking entertainment or information, for better or worse, there was no doubt that England had become a reading nation.

Strong though the bonds of leisure at home were, the powerful calls of outside entertainment could not be resisted, and never before had there been such a range from which to choose. Improved transport in the shape of better roads, railways, horse-buses, and later electric-trams brought an ever-widening circle of spectators and participants, which in turn created more and different entertainments.

For those who wished to continue their violent exercise indoors there were 'real' Tennis and its offsprings, Squash and Fives, but none of these had a wide appeal outside the upper and middle classes. A new game of a similar type was 'discovered' about 1870, when, it is said, the Duke of Beaufort tried to play 'real' Tennis in the picture-gallery of his house at Badminton, but found that oil paintings of his ancestors suffered in the process. Whether that is true or not, the game we know as Badminton did evolve at the Duke's home from an Indian sport known as Poona. When played indoors a shuttle was used to prevent damage, but out of doors a rubber ball was substituted as the shuttle was too light. The fast, energetic game remained rather limited in appeal until the last years of the century when its delights suddenly dawned, and it became a well-established sport.

More popular than the bat-and-ball games with the ordinary people was Roller-skating. In most parts of Britain good bearing ice was all too rare for skating out of doors ever to become a major sport as it was on the Continent, but the grace and ease of the skater when he did get a chance to show his skill made a great impression on the minds of the people. Many attempts had been made to manufacture a land-skate— or roller-skate—in the eighteenth century, but none had been entirely successful until the 1850's when the modern four-wheeled device was introduced. Within a few years every town worthy of the name had a rink, sometimes indoors in a converted hall or public building with a wooden floor but more often merely a flat concrete or asphalt surface surrounded by a fence. Occasionally there was a bandstand in the centre, and for hours on end the crowds clanked their noisy, dusty way round it to the blare of trumpet and trombone.

But at best Roller-skating was a poor substitute for the real thing, and the search for perfection went on. In 1842 a rink had been opened in London in which the 'ice' consisted of certain chemicals mixed with pig's lard, but the surface was too soft for prolonged use so the business failed.

During the next twenty-five years inventors made great advances in machines for refrigeration, and in 1877 an indoor rink of real ice was opened in Manchester at immense cost. Most surprisingly this, together with a similar one at Southport, failed completely to attract the public, and had to close a year or two later. It was well into the twentieth century before indoor Ice-skating achieved the popularity it has to-day.

The public amusements so far mentioned were more for the young and vigorous: those beyond the energetic age wanted to be entertained rather than to entertain themselves by chasing tiny balls or hurling their bodies at breakneck speed round a concrete or wooden floor. They had a wide choice, and it is not surprising in view of the popularity of music in the home that concerts were high on the list. London had many halls devoted to serious music, the Crystal Palace, the Royal Albert Hall, and Queen's Hall being the most famous, while Manchester led the way among the provincial towns with its Hallé Orchestra, founded in 1857.

The North of England, especially Lancashire and Yorkshire, was perhaps more genuinely inspired by a love of music than most of the south, for almost all of the towns, and even some of the factories, had their own brass bands which competed against each other at gigantic festivals. Hundreds of thousands of people from all ranks of life in the textile towns who could play no instrument met several times a week to sing together for the sheer joy of it, or to rehearse for the great event of their year— the public performance of *Messiah* or one of the other great oratorios.

For those whose musical taste did not run on such high levels as symphonies, operas, or oratorios, the public pleasure-gardens, especially those at Vauxhall in London, still offered light music for all who cared to pay the shilling entrance fee. Lower still on the musical scale were the German bands who, with trombones, trumpets, and big drums, paraded the streets during the summer months collecting as they went. On the very bottom rung were the organ-grinders—usually Italian—with their hired tinkling machines, their begging red-capped monkeys, and the usual crowd of chattering children.

In the nineteenth century the theatre completely regained its respectability, particularly when Queen Victoria showed by her visits how much she enjoyed it, and the great popularity of drama at all levels was reflected in the improvements which took place.

From the very early days of the theatre it had been a law that only Covent Garden and Drury Lane were allowed to play 'straight' drama, all other theatres being allowed to give musical or dancing shows or other light entertainment only. Many of these 'minor' theatres had, of course, for years avoided this stupid restriction by putting song or dance interludes into ordinary plays, but after 1843, when the law was repealed, they were no longer forced to adopt such roundabout methods.

In the years so much given to mechanical things it is not surprising that the most remarkable changes in the theatre were not connected with the plays themselves but with the machinery and equipment. Gas, which could be controlled from a single tap to give just the right amount of light required, was installed early in the century, and was thought the height of perfection until, in the 1880's, electricity was first used. Scenery was hoisted into the roof by cranes, trapdoors opened here and there, and often the backcloth revolved horizontally on rollers to give the impression of movement for race scenes. The theatre, backstage, was beginning to resemble an engineer's nightmare as well as a dramatist's.

The movement begun in the eighteenth century to clothe actors in the correct historical costume continued, and with so many more people able to study books it went ill with a producer whose dress or scenery was incorrect. Yet in the struggle for technical improvement the audience was not forgotten, and the improved comforts offered helped to swell the takings. The hard wooden benches, at least in the more expensive parts of the theatre, were replaced by comfortably upholstered seating, and towards the end of the century heating was installed.

Shakespeare's plays were still the main diet of the serious theatregoer, though dramatized versions of popular novels, especially Dickens, were highly successful. Melodramas were riotously popular, particularly with less-educated audiences who hissed and booed the moustached villain as he was foiled at the last moment by the hero rescuing the fainting heroine from her dreadful fate. Other melodramas were glamorized accounts of particularly horrifying murders in which justice always finally triumphed, while still others depicted the downward path of the drunkard until at the end of a play usually well sprinkled with tragic deaths he was converted from his wicked ways. In the latter half of the century, however, theatregoers had a much wider choice, a number of excellent comedies of manners and serious plays dealing with problems of the moment filling the wide gap between *King Lear* and *Maria Marten, or the Murder in the Red Barn.*

As to-day, the permanent theatres had to be situated in large cities, and usually then in the more central areas. Millions of people living in small towns, country districts, and even in the more remote slums and suburbs of the big cities themselves would have had few opportunities of coming into contact with drama of any kind had it not been for the 'penny gaff.'

These were companies of actors, perhaps not of the first rank, who travelled the country setting up temporary theatres, sometimes in disused shops or halls in the towns, or, in the more isolated districts, in marquees. The crowded, sweating, chewing audience, usually drawn from the emotional and poorer sections of the population, booed, hissed, cheered, and wept with complete abandon at the broad melodramas which were the main offering of this type of theatre, although Shakespeare's plays were seen quite frequently. The audiences, who probably would have understood little of the original classics, were equally delighted with *Hamlet* and *Maria Marten*, possibly because the actors, while sticking fairly closely to the plots, helped out Shakespeare's more difficult passages with lines of their own creation.

Some companies made a boast of making a three- or four-week stand, and giving nightly performances without repeating a single item—no mean feat when almost every member of the troupe was involved in each play. The shows were given on crude stages with crude lighting and even cruder scenery, and each actor kept almost exclusively to his or her own type of rôle—villain, heroine, comic, or child. Thus Macbeth on Monday would appear as Sweeney Todd, the Demon Barber, on Tuesday, and as the drunkard on Wednesday. Rough and ready though they were, the travelling theatres did bring at least a glimmering of the drama into lives which otherwise would have known none at all, and it is a great pity that our twentieth-century slick sophistication and the high standards set by radio and television have driven these live shows out of existence.

Yet of all the memories of the theatre which linger from Victoria's reign, the strongest is that of the pantomime, the highlight—for the children, at least—of the long, dark winter months. The audiences of the 1800's were greedy—or perhaps they just liked value for money—for all theatres were forced to give at least one, and often two, short plays or entertainments besides the main item on the programme. Four-hour performances were quite usual, and as the ballets and harlequinades of the eighteenth century were so popular, they had to be lengthened. To give the exhausted dancers a rest, clowning-interludes were introduced. Gradually the fairy-story round which the Harlequin and Colombine and dancing revolved merged with the comic element to give the mammoth Victorian pantomime, which became a feat of endurance, with a dozen or more glittering scenes.

The evening fell into two parts divided by the great climax of the whole show—the transformation scene. The first part worked steadily through one of the hundreds of fairy-stories, and when the wedding or whatever the happy ending happened to be was reached the Fairy Queen waved her wand. Amid a thrill of expectancy and a whirr of machinery, the whole stage changed from winter to summer or from earth to fairyland as the characters of the legend became Harlequin, Columbine, Pantaloon, and the rest. The second half of the evening consisted of clowning and dancing, but by then a good part of the youthful audiences was far too weary to appreciate it.

By 1880 a strong love-story had become established in pantomime, probably as an offering to the adults, and of the myriads of fables and legends originally acted, only the half-dozen or so we see to-day were being used. All the elements we enjoy to-day—the topical songs, the men in women's parts, and women in men's, and the specialist acts—had become traditional in what was exclusively a British entertainment.

Perhaps the most typical and most loved after-dark amusement of Victorian England was the music-hall, a bouncing child whose father was the inn and whose mother was the theatre. Taverns had found from an early date that some form of entertainment for their customers encouraged them to eat and drink more than they had intended, and by the nineteenth century the idea had been really developed. A large room filled with tables for the diners was fitted with a platform at one end, and beside this, often on a dais, was the chairman's seat. The meals served were usually of a light nature, though the drink was not, and to the accompaniment of clattering cutlery, chinking glasses, and the scurrying of waiters busy with orders, the chairman would rap with his mallet on the table for silence to announce the next performers.

Most of the turns were songs, usually a verse of jingle with a tuneful, catchy, nonsensical chorus in which the customers joined with crumby and alcoholic vigour. Patriotic and excessively sentimental songs were also well received, and the programme, announced item by item by the chairman, often included conjuring, acrobatic, and impersonation acts. In some of the larger halls high-wire artistes performed in the body of the building above the dining-tables. The music-halls were robust, noisy, and cheerfully intimate, and when towards the end of the period, many

A music-hall

of them moved to specially built theatres with a proper stage and auditorium, a printed programme and no chairman, much of the warm cordiality and informal atmosphere disappeared.

Many of the new types of entertainment that burst on the nineteenth century had their roots deep in the past, and this was very true of the circus. From the Dark Ages performing animals, acrobats, rope-walkers, had travelled the country individually giving shows for a living, but not until the early nineteenth century were these performers organized into a composite show under one roof.

A certain ex-Sergeant Major Astley began it all in 1770 when he opened a riding-school in London after a successful army career. He soon discovered that displays of horsemanship and trick-riding were much more profitable than teaching pupils how to sit their saddles properly, and devoted his arena entirely to this side of his business. When in 1780 the theatre was rebuilt with candle lighting for evening performances and a stage for dancing and musical interludes the real circus was born. Astley's in Westminster Bridge Road became a goal for amusement-seekers, despite the fact that it was destroyed by fire in 1794 and again in 1803. But on each occasion a new 'Astley's' emerged from the ashes.

Rival arenas naturally sprang up, and the race for the public was on. To keep ahead of the field, Astley's introduced their immensely popular Military and Equestrian Dramas—representations of battles, fights, and other dramatic scenes in which horses could be introduced. They must have been rather like battle scenes in a modern searchlight tattoo on a much smaller scale, and until the arena was sold to become an ordinary theatre in 1863, its only real rival in the minds of children was the Christmas pantomime.

Some of the competitors who arrived late on the scene realized that their only hope of success was to take to the road, and soon the tiny travelling-circus began to make its appearance at fairs as a sideshow. Most of these were very small indeed, consisting of three or four horses, a clown, an acrobat, and perhaps a rope-walker, and, with the tent sandwiched between that of the bearded lady and the booth of the two-headed calf, they gave shows whenever the proprietor thought he had an audience large enough.

It was not long before the owners of the wild-beast shows and menageries and the circus proprietors saw that it would be advantageous to join forces to make a show which could move independently of the fairs. Very soon the circus and menagerie, with its horse-drawn caravans and cages, its brass band, and parade of the more docile animals, was travelling up and down the country giving regular performances.

Soon after the middle of the century some circuses were having their equipment drawn along the roads by lumbering steam-engines, and these snorting monsters, particularly in country districts, often proved a stronger attraction than the show itself, for their performance was free.

In the eighties English enthusiasts were treated to a new delight when Buffalo Bill Cody brought his Wild West Show from America, the home of the mammoth circus. His spectacular presentations showed that many of our own companies had got into a rut, and pricked them into great efforts to find new acts. Sangers' Circus in particular soon became a fierce rival of the transatlantic show, combining the traditional and well-loved 'battle' episodes with the more modern, faster type of entertainment.

But even the mightiest circus was to bow before a new pastime which came to the public of the United States the first time in 1894 and to England two years later. No one realized then when watching the first, flickering, jerking, three-minute moving-pictures that within thirty-five years the cinema would completely dominate the whole field of public indoor entertainment.

The earliest films were shown as novelties at music-halls and fairs, and mere movement satisfied the viewers, who were quite content to pay to see a blurred train run into a station, a hazy horse jump over a fence, or even a man jerk like a clockwork-toy across a room. If the Moving Pictures had remained thus they would, as every one thought, have died an early death, but in the very last years of the century the screen began to tell a story. At first the plot was very simple—robbers chased and caught by police, all in two minutes—but like the drama in the church five hundred years earlier, the cinema captured the imagination of the public. Pushed by terrific popular pressure, the film soon left its humble beginnings in the fairground and became an entertainment in its own right: within fifteen or sixteen years of its first introduction crowds were thronging into darkened halls to feast on full-length shows of comedy, tragedy, history, or even the Scriptures.

Although there was such a wide range of clean, civilized, harmless amusement, even if some of it was not of great cultural value, there were still the few who sought out the old, cruel, savage sports of their fathers. In country districts and in the slums of the cities the blood sports still claimed a following, and while it was impossible to bait bulls or bears after the law forbidding it in 1835, Cockfighting was easy to conceal. The law of 1849 in any case prohibited only public mains, and even then promoters often thought that the profits they would make were well worth the maximum fine of £5. But like Dog-fighting and Rat-killing contests, the cockfights appealed only to a very small minority and those of the very lowest.

Prize-fighting with bare fists, although officially illegal, drew larger crowds to the so-called secret meetings despite the fact that all decent people were disgusted with the bloody maulings which constituted most of the matches. Sometimes for over a hundred rounds or two or three hours' battering, the courageous but senseless opponents would beat each other to semiconscious pulp while the dregs of the community screamed themselves hoarse or started free fights among themselves. The matches which had in the eighteenth century been purely local affairs now drew the scum from miles around by means of the railway.

Despite this, however, knuckle-fighting was itself fighting a losing battle, and finally sealed its career in 1860 with the famous match between the British champion, Sayers, and the American, Heenan, at Farnborough. For nearly two hours and a half the pair battled, Sayers for most of the time with a broken bone in his arm, and when as both men were tottering with exhaustion, the result was declared a draw, the mob broke into a pitched battle. Apart from a few local bouts, that was the end: Prize-fighting had run its course. The gap which had been left in the British sporting picture was soon filled when Lord Queensberry, in 1865, drew up the rules under which Boxing takes place to-day. For the last forty years of the century padded gloves, the canvas ring, and three-minute rounds with one minute intervals, restored fighting as a clean, healthy sport in its own right, and as such drew its supporters from labourers and lords, dustmen and dukes.

All of the diversions and recreations so far discussed have been of short duration—a few hours at most—and could be squeezed easily into the evening or the very rare day or half-day of holiday from work. No one in the earlier part of the century had even considered that the ordinary working-people needed a rest from their twelve or more hours a day in the factories and mills. Sundays, Christmas Day, and Good Friday were the usual breaks from labour, and very often not even these were observed. Most employers did not, or would not, believe that the increased tempo of life and the conditions of work, shackled to a machine that did not give a breathing space from morning till night, absolutely demanded a rest occasionally.

The first step in releasing the people from semi-slavery was taken by the Government in 1833 when the first Factory Act laid down that all children under eighteen years of age must have eight-and-a-half days' holiday a year in addition to Christmas and Good Friday. Although the Law was often disobeyed, it did on the whole benefit grown-ups as well for children were such a vital part of industry that the factories could not continue with their particular machines out of operation. There was no suggestion, of course, that the workers should be paid while they were on holiday, and this was an important factor, for most people just could not afford to lose the wages. With only one person in fifty earning more than £2 a week there was little enough after essentials had been bought to put by for holidays.

Yet kindliness was in the air, and after the middle of the century one employer after another began to make concessions to his workers. The weekly half-day, usually Saturday afternoon, became general in factories and industry, though shop assistants had to work even harder with the extra customers swarming the streets. After about 1880 too more and more people, especially those in offices and shops, began to be given pay while they were on holiday, a period usually of one or two weeks.

In 1871 Sir John Lubbock managed to get a cleverly disguised Bill through Parliament which gave every one in the country at least four days a year of liberty from work—the bank holidays of Boxing Day, Easter Monday, Whit Monday, and August Monday. Together with Christmas Day and Good Friday, this ensured that almost every one had a few breaks spaced fairly regularly throughout the year to relieve the monotony.

Throughout the century, then, the whole of England enjoyed more and more leisure, ranging from the unpaid, compulsory four days of the meanest employers, through the paid three weeks of the generous ones, to the almost permanent luxurious holiday of the wealthiest. This set a great problem: how was the new-won spare time to be spent. Many, of

M

course, enjoyed themselves locally at sports, races, fairs, or picnicking, but for an ever-growing majority the answer was the seaside.

For millions of people the highlight of the year, the sole reason for the holiday, was the trip to the coast. Without it, the summer was wasted. For the poor worker the day excursion had to suffice, but the better-paid artisan often managed a week while the middle class stayed for a fortnight or even longer. The aristocracy and wealthy families retreated before the invasion of their resorts by what they considered the lower orders to spend their summer holidays in Scotland, Ireland, the Lake District or abroad, but nothing could stop the meteoric growth of the seaside towns.

There is little doubt that the seaside holiday for ordinary people owed its existence entirely to the steam-engine, for as the railway-lines or steamboats reached tiny coastal villages at once they began to burst their seams during the summer months. Blackpool, for example, could claim only about eight hundred visitors at the height of the season in the 1830's while most of the South-coast towns apart from Brighton had less than a hundred. Ten years later the number of holidaymakers was running into four and five figures.

The resorts within a few hours run in a paddle-steamer of the big cities—towns such as Margate and Southend on the Thames, the North Wales villages near Liverpool and those villages along the Clyde—first felt the rush of holidaymakers and trippers in the twenties and thirties, but the expansion of the railway in the years 1840 to 1850 enabled the pleasure-seekers to travel farther and farther afield.

If there had been any doubts they were quickly settled by two important events in the history of holidays which took place in the 1840's. The first was an Act which compelled every railway-line to run at least one train a day stopping at every station and charging one penny a mile—about a quarter of the fare charged by the stage-coaches— and secondly, the excursion train with fares even less than those of the 'Parliamentary Train.' For the excursion two famous men were responsible—for very different reasons. Sir Rowland Hill, the originator of the penny post and chairman of the Brighton Railway, began very cheap trips to the coast to make profit for his company, and Thomas Cook, a working man who founded the well-known travel agency, and a great campaigner against alcohol, organized trains to take his supporters very cheaply to Temperance meetings.

From these small beginnings the excursion spread like wildfire to

Bathing-machine modesty hoods

school parties, church outings, and trips organized by societies and good
employers for their workpeople. Not only was there the dangerous thrill
of being hurtled through the air in the open truck at a terrifying twenty-
five miles an hour, but also the long day on the shore, and then the roar
homeward with the iron monster ahead in the darkness belching orange
flame and showers of soot to add a finishing touch to the day's layer of
grime on the weary but happy travellers.

And what exactly did the countless thousands do when they had
reached the coast for their few hours or few weeks?

There were first of all the changeless joys of nature—the fresh, clean
air and spaciousness after the smoke and jumble of the city, the fascinating
noise and pattern of the waves, rocks and cliffs to be climbed, sand to
be dug, and countless myriads of pebbles to be hurled out to sea. Then
there was the bathing. For the whole of the century the big horse-drawn
bathing-machines dominated the seaside scene, and from these emerged
the men (nude until the 1860's) and women (in bathing-costumes
reaching from the chin to wrists and ankles) to sport themselves—
separately—in the waves. To make the swim even more private many
machines had a huge hood which completely covered the bather from
the time she left the door until she was in the water. The dippers of the
eighteenth century lingered well on into the nineteenth, much to the
disgust of reluctant children who suffered at their hands, though these
could not really be considered attractions of the seaside.

Bathing on Sunday was not approved by the strict Victorians, and
at Brighton on one occasion a number of ladies, suitably clad in the
Sabbath black, seated themselves in front of the machines which a
number of gentlemen had used for undressing. We are not told how long
the grim band kept their naked, shivering, and blue victims up to their
chins in the water.

When the natural enjoyments of the seaside had been exhausted
the holidaymaker turned to the man-made ones, on the beach, on the
promenade, and on that most English of inventions, the pier.

No resort worth its salt was without its string of donkeys who plodded
their reluctant and bored way across the sands with a constant procession
of children on their backs. For adults there were horses and ponies,
usually of poor quality, for hire, and the gentle amble on both these
and the donkeys became in imagination the most wild and heroic of
gallops in the same way as the trip round a glassy bay in a rowing-boat

The Ethiopians, or Nigger Minstrels

propelled by a seasoned old fisherman became a real adventure on the high seas.

Less thrilling, but equally delightful, were the Punch and Judy shows and their adult counterparts, the Ethiopian Serenaders. Punch and his wickedness have not changed or grown a day older since Victorian times, but the Ethiopians, apart from rare appearances as Kentucky Minstrels on the radio and television, have gone. For many years after their introduction from America about 1850 they were, however, one of the most popular and most evident attractions of the seaside.

The Ethiopians, or Nigger Minstrels, worked sometimes in small groups of two or three round the holidaymakers seated on the beach, or at other times a larger party charged admission to a small open-air theatre on the sand. Dressed in long white trousers, coloured cut-away jackets, large bow-ties, and top-hats, and with their faces blackened with burnt cork, they strummed ceaselessly on their banjos. Their entertainment consisted of nostalgic plantation songs, comic ditties, often with a rollicking chorus, and rapid gabble of cross-talk, in what was supposed to be the accents of the American negro, between Sambo, Bones, and Mr Interlocutor.

Noisy though they were, the Ethiopians added only a small part to the constant clangor that seemed one of the major joys of the seaside. Their twanging and chattering merged into the general din of blaring German brass bands, wailing fiddle bands, tinkling hurdy-gurdies and music-boxes, and the raucous yelling of donkey-boys, bathchair attendants, and proprietors of food-and-drink stalls. Harps, bagpipes, and occasionally even pianos on trolleys lent a variation to the general hubbub.

The pier, if one chose a time when the resident brass band was not playing, did offer a slight escape from the hurly-burly of the beach and promenade. There one could fish, of course, but that wasted too much time for the day-tripper who had to pack into half a dozen hours all of the more exciting amusements. Then there were telescopes which for a penny gave a few minutes' view of the distant lighthouse or a ship on the horizon, and weighing-machines which as early as 1839 were offering a card printed with the date and the customer's weight.

At the end of the pier the camera obscura could usually be found, inviting and mysterious. This was a darkened room containing a large circular white table on which, by means of lenses and mirrors, was thrown the image, in full colours and full motion, of the beach and promenade. One could occasionally pick out one's friends, and this was all the more fun if they were at the moment doing something they wished might not be known.

There were stalls of food, drink, souvenirs, and sweets, and when the leaden protesting legs refused to move another step, there were the hard wooden benches—no deckchairs—from the comfort of which one could watch the rest of the world nervously exhausting itself in sampling the delights of the seaside.

While the excursionist and tripper scurried to and fro in a frenzied effort to taste all of the more obvious joys, the quieter, calmer pleasures of the holiday were reserved for those whose stay lasted a week or more. Foremost among these delights, at least for children, was collecting shells. Huge bagfuls of all sizes and colours would be treasured on the homeward journey and saved for the long winter evenings when, with the help of a little barbola paste, they recaptured some of summer's delights as they were made into picture-frames, ornaments, and pin-trays.

Few parents knew much of the science of shells so that this fun was free of the cloud which sometimes lingered over scrambling in and out of rock pools. Even on holiday Victorian parents could not help mixing a little education with enjoyment so that pools often became lessons in nature-study with the life-habits of anemones, shrimps, and other tiny creatures laid bare. Rocks and cliffs, though always tremendously thrilling, had the danger of bringing out a tiny hammer and a geology lecture.

Trips by carriage to local beauty-spots and places of interest were always a feature when the first joys of the beach began to tarnish a little, and for girls who were too old to romp in the sand and yet were not admitted to adults' pleasures there were countless subjects for the ever-present water-colours. For wet days, and when every other source had been exhausted, there was always Mudie's lending-library, branches of which sprang up as each resort was added to the list.

Many resorts had facilities for sports and games but Croquet and later Lawn Tennis were by far the most popular as one would expect from the leisurely, holiday way in which they can be played. It had taken Britons eighteen centuries to discover the seaside, but when they did there is no doubt that they threw themselves wholeheartedly into the task of screwing every atom of pleasure from it.

Serious-minded and severe though Victorian parents may have been on holiday, and indeed at all times, there is no doubt that they deeply loved their children: the vast number of toys that were invented and bought amply demonstrates this if there were no other evidence. It is equally obvious too that children had never in history been so well catered for in the matter of manufactured amusements—perhaps the grown-ups felt pangs of guilty conscience about the compulsory schooling they had introduced in 1870, and made some attempt at compensation.

Although adults for most of the nineteenth century had little use for mechanization in their pastimes, children's toys were mechanical from the very beginning. Clockwork, gravity, sand, spinning-flywheels and later steam, all provided the driving-power for hundreds of ingenious and delightful models which struggled to get themselves included under the Victorian heading of Useful or Instructive Toys.

Some toys of course, such as balls, tops, and the like, could in no wise be classed as educational, but as a rule it was insisted that a pastime should first teach and secondly amuse. Manufacturers eased their consciences by advertising that the latest novelty would instruct in arithmetic, history, geography, or even astronomy or philosophy, but, alas, the children all too often delighted in the game for its own sake, and were completely unaware of what they were supposed to learn.

Simplest and most direct of the educational entertainments were the board and card games which had got off to such a good start in the previous century. Every conceivable type of 'race' game in which counters moved from place to place under the throws of dice or spinning of a teetotum were devised, but historical and geographical ones led as they were perhaps the simplest to make up. There were board and card games to teach French, spelling, arithmetic, various sciences, and good manners, while jigsaw puzzles, still simple and not interlocking, concentrated on Scripture knowledge, with history and geography a poor second and third. With such a spate of instruction in the nursery it is a wonder that children had anything to learn from their teachers, or indeed that schooling needed to be compulsory at all.

More subtle in their educational approach were the scientific toys which claimed to teach the laws of nature. There was, for example, a whole range of equipment to instruct in the rather obscure science of optics, but not one child in a thousand gave a thought to the laws of light and reflection when he was absorbed in the three-dimensional pictures in his stereoscope or the patterns in his kaleidoscope. The magic lantern was a glutton for work, for its job of tuition was like Morton's Fork. If the child missed one set of teaching it was caught on the other, for besides illustrating the principles of lenses on which the lantern worked, the handcoloured slides were usually of historical, geographical, or Scriptural subjects. Only occasionally did the stern manufacturers relax and produce something light-hearted such as the moving-slide. One such example threw on the screen a picture of a greedy little boy seated at a table on which stood a steaming round Christmas-pudding. At the touch of the lever a part of the slide moved so that the pudding and boy's head changed places, the head appearing on the dish and the pudding on the boy's shoulders.

Most famous of all the optical toys were the zoetrope, phenakistescope, and their many variations which were the real forerunners of the cinema. Through a series of slots in a revolving drum or disc one could see a tiny figure apparently in motion, performing simple operations such as skipping, running, juggling, or catching plums in its mouth. They showed the one operation over and over again, but in some of the devices extra slips of paper printed with the figures could be bought to clip inside so that a fresh animated picture could be viewed.

To show the lengths that manufacturers and shopkeepers went to to find an educational excuse for their wares, peashooters were sometimes sold as demonstrating the principles of compressed air.

Power-driven toys burst on a delighted children's world, first of all from the German factories and then towards the end of the century from the British ones. Trains, which figured so largely in adult life, were an obvious choice, and as early as 1840 tiny, tin, clockwork-powered engines and their trucks were scratching their way up and down the polished parlour-tables. Roundabouts, walking animals, race games, and moving figures all with tiny spring-operated motors poured in endless variety from the workshops as the century progressed, completely bewildering parents who were hard-pressed to find any serious purpose behind their aimless mechanical movements.

Some moving toys were worked by sand which fell from a hopper at the top of the model on a miniature waterwheel, which in turn caused the sails of a windmill or the arms of an organ-grinder on the front of the box, which enclosed the apparatus, to revolve. Other toys, usually tumblers or acrobats, were partially filled with mercury which caused them to lurch and wobble amusingly down slopes or steps. Both the sand and quicksilver models were sometimes optimistically advertised as explaining the laws of gravity to children.

Elastic was occasionally used to propel simple animals figures across the floor or table, but far more popular as a motor was the spinning-flywheel. Spun by a piece of string, rather like the modern gyroscope toy, the flywheel drove, through gearing, cyclists, horsemen, or perhaps foot-racers suspended on the end of pieces of stiff wire round and round the central tin huts which housed the driving mechanism. Often two figures were driven independently and so arranged that until they finally stopped no one could tell which was going to win. But most delightful of all were the flywheel toys in which the wheel was hidden or disguised as part of the model: in a pair of dancers, for example, the bottom hem of the lady's crinoline was the edge of the wheel, so that the couple glided round and round, seemingly quite on their own. In another such toy which showed an elephant with an Indian prince on its back the flywheel was the rajah's elaborate umbrella open above his head.

Playthings for girls have always tended to be severely practical, fitting them for their future lives as housewives and mothers. The nineteenth century was no exception, and rather than any marked change as there had been for boys with their mechanical pastimes, girls' toys showed a greater abundance and range.

Dolls and their equipment have always been the spearhead of the female nursery, and dolls there were in Victorian times of every material, price, and degree of elaboration, ranging from the cheapest rag or wooden figure to the exquisite china ones. Most dolls had a cloth body stuffed with sawdust, to which was added a head, and sometimes hands and feet, of the substance then in the fashion. In the early part of the century wax was the most popular, but was followed in the forties and fifties by papier-mâché. Then followed china, from which beautifully delicate features could be made but which was very fragile indeed, and finally bisque, a manufactured substance more durable than china.

On the very best dolls' heads, particularly in the wax period, the eyelashes and hairs were inserted one by one, an expensive but most realistic process. Movable eyes were introduced early in the century, the first ones being operated by means of a wire protruding from the body. Later on the automatic 'sleeping' system was invented. Rather surprisingly to the modern girl, almost all of the dolls were adults, the 'baby' not becoming at all popular until the end of the century.

With the improved dolls naturally came a mass of improved equipment. Clothing could be bought ready-made, but far more worthy in Victorian eyes were the sewing outfits with which every girl could make her own 'family's' wardrobe. Dolls' houses were no longer joys known only to the wealthy child, for if fathers or big brothers could not be persuaded to make one from the many designs given in the practical magazines and papers, there were cheap factory-made buildings. Furniture of cardboard could be bought for a copper or two, but often there was no necessity for any expense at all, for almost every item could be improvised from empty matchboxes and other forms of packaging as goods flooded into the shops. Tea and dinner services ranged from the perfect miniatures in porcelain to crude, cheap, painted tin plate. Cutlery, fire-irons, and general household equipment might be of wood, card, or any metal, including silver.

The Victorian housewife, whether she was to have a dozen servants or none at all, was expected to know not only how to run the home, manage children, and entertain guests but also how to buy and cook the food. What more delightful way of introducing her to such tasks was there than the toy kitchens which had become so popular in the previous century and the tiny wooden or card shops where she could buy the plaster of Paris joints of meat, vegetables, fruit, and sweetmeat groceries of all kinds, and at the same time acquire invaluable market knowledge.

The young lady's dress sense was not forgotten either. For a few pence could be bought a figure in stiff cardboard mounted on a wooden base with sheets of printed dresses, coats, hats, and accessories for cutting out and fitting by means of tabs over the shoulders of the model. Occasionally the figures were of men, but the drab colours and dull styles which reigned in masculine wear for most of the century did not stand a chance with the rapidly and most dramatically changing clothing of the ladies.

Yet there were some toys which remained even to the Victorians just pure fun, and many of these were games which appealed to both boys and girls alike. Among the outdoor amusements in this category were tops of all varieties, hoops—wooden for girls and iron for boys, Tipcat, Marbles, and 'crazes' such as Diabolo. This last game, which had a riotous popularity towards the end of the century, is occasionally seen to-day and consists of two cones, joined tip to tip, which are made to run back and forth along a piece of string tied to two sticks and held in the hands. As the skill of the operator increased, spectacular tricks could be performed.

Children's games underwent a minor revolution in the middle of the century with the coming into use of rubber balls. These were not only cheaper but also much better than the stuffed solid ones, and whereas for hundreds of years throwing and catching had been the basis of all games, now bouncing began to open up new avenues, particularly for a child on its own. Out of doors too there was a craze, inspired no doubt by the daring descents from balloons, for Parachuting. Pieces of string from the four corners of a handkerchief were fastened to a stone or piece of iron, and then the whole apparatus was hurled high into the air to drift gently to earth. As telephone wires did not appear in any great number until the end of the century, these aerial toys of the nineteenth century were free from the danger that besets so many of them to-day.

It was difficult to attach any real educational value to toy soldiers, either, but they were always a favourite, particularly after 1860 when a British firm invented hollow models in place of the flat wooden or metal ones from Germany which had held the field for so long. As the small-scale wars in different parts of the Empire broke out, the appropriate warriors, such as Zulus or Boers, soon appeared in the shops for boys to re-enact their fathers' battles. In the last ten years of the century, probably owing much to Buffalo Bill's Wild West Show from America, two new armies poured from the toyshops to the floor battlefields—cowboys and Indians and all their equipment.

Less liable to lead to real battles in the nursery were building blocks and bricks. Some of these were simple cubes brightly coloured and bearing the letters of the alphabet on the faces, and which were really in the educational class; others contained rectangular, triangular, and cylindrical blocks and archways so that more realistic houses and churches could be built. Elementary constructional sets consisting of flat strips of wood about five inches long and three-quarters of an inch wide, slotted at both ends so they could slip together, managed to squeeze in the last years of the period, heralding the way for such complicated and wonderful toys as " Meccano " in our own century.

There were even board games which set out to teach children nothing but to smile—Ludo, for example, was invented in 1896, but the card game in which the most amazing faces or figures could be created had a much longer run. Each card in the set bore the drawing of a different person or face, and was divided into three parts. By shuffling the strips and getting a man's head on, say, a gorilla's body with an ostrich's legs, the most uproarious results could follow, particularly if it had been decided beforehand that the next picture was to represent Mr So-and-So.

In a class all by itself, and possibly the most outstanding indoor pastime for children of much of the Victorian age, was the toy theatre. Little stages could be bought ready-made, but these were not half as much fun as the card ones which needed cutting out and glueing together. Tiny tin candle-holders and other stage manager's equipment could be obtained, and when all was ready hours were spent in the toyshop choosing the actors for the first play.

These were printed on sheets of paper or card, sometimes just outlines, others already coloured (penny plain, and twopenny coloured), and had to be cut out and clipped into a clip at the end of a tin slide. Each sheet contained all the characters and properties for one play or pantomime— and there were hundreds from which to choose. For the first few shows, when the youthful producer could not wait to get his cardboard actors moving about the stage, coloured sheets were usually bought, but the more experienced and wiser managers bought the plain ones, for painting them occupied many more happy hours.

With theatre and players ready, the family, if they could be so persuaded, were driven into the darkened drawing-room, with the flimsy candle-lit stage standing on the table. The paper figures slid woodenly up and down or flashed in fierce duels while the operators behind chanted the speeches, well punctuated with giggles, silences, and "go on's."

More advanced performers could stage quite impressive tricks such as real explosions and fires, but all too often when those not so skilled attempted these the whole theatre and characters went up in flames. Even if no such dangerous spectacles were being attempted the guttering candles or a jolted table often resulted in the same fate, and scorched furniture must have caused thousands of the miniature theatres to be banished, if not from the home completely, at least to the hours of daylight, which was not half as exciting.

Fortunate though children were, however, Sunday tended to be rather a dull day, for in many homes even the educational games were locked away. Scripture jigsaws might be allowed, and so might boxes of cardboard letters, provided only texts were made with them. Religious slides in the magic lantern could not be permitted as there was always the optical side to be considered. For the youngest Noah's Ark with its Biblical connexions might be allowed, but in houses as strict as these there would have been little time for play of any sort between the regular visits to church or chapel.

So the Victorians, adults and children, amused themselves, and although they had so much less free time than we have to-day, they probably took their leisure much more leisurely, savouring their enjoyments to the full. In the midst of organizing and running the greatest Empire the world had known, and turning a tiny island into the industrial and commercial centre of the globe, they found time to lay the foundations of almost all of our modern recreations. It is true we have developed some and modified others so that the nineteenth century would hardly recognize them, but the roots are there. What can we in the twentieth century claim to have introduced in major sports and recreations that compares with Football, Rugby, Hockey, Tennis, Rowing, Athletics, the Cinema, the music-hall, the seaside, and mechanical toys? Our fame rests at the moment on the broad shoulders of radio and television, and no one can blame the nineteenth century for not having the scientific knowledge to create those.

CHAPTER VIII

American Sports

THE story of leisure in North America is very much like that of Britain except that it is speeded up and compressed into three-and-a-half centuries instead of fifteen. In the first half of the seventeenth century the pressure of hostile surroundings and of work made the early colonists' position rather similar to that of the Saxons in the sixth century; by 1850 the American and his British counterpart were enjoying very similar pleasures, while to-day many people think the citizen of the New World is far ahead of his Old World brother in the matter of leisure.

All this in three hundred and fifty years! But the reasons are not hard to find. The immense natural wealth of America and her vast spaciousness have paid for and encouraged recreation. The courage and quality of the first settlers mingled with the national characteristics of the immigrants who poured from every corner of the known world to form a new race free from many of the worn-out ideas of the old world, and, finally, the very different reasons which drew men to the great unknown, challenging land—religion, trade, adventure, and curiosity—were bound to stimulate development of every aspect of life, including leisure.

Before the white man crossed the Atlantic life for the native Indians was poor and hard—unnecessarily so in a land of such plenty. Much of his time was spent in wresting from nature enough to live, and most of the remainder in fighting the neighbouring tribe to protect what he had won. But even so, there must have been occasions when peace and plenty coincided and some relaxation was demanded. As with most primitive races, there was no doubt a grim pleasure in the fearsome religious dances and festivals, but there were other amusements too. One author has suggested that the Indians of the plains played a gruesome game of football, using the heads of enemies as the ball, but while this is probably untrue, it is certain that the game which gave rise to the modern Lacrosse is of North American origin. Baggataway, as the Indians called it, consisted of hurling a ball to and fro with the aid of nets on the ends of long poles to goals miles apart. Sometimes the game was used as an alternative to more bloodthirsty battles between tribes, hundreds on each side taking part, but as it was the custom of the womenfolk to urge their men on by beating them with cudgels, the braves probably found Baggataway little less dangerous than the more normal warfare.

In the hot and arid south the Indians sought more peaceful pastimes, and, squatting in the sun, played one of the race games of which the following is typical.

Forty small stones were placed in a ring about four feet in diameter, with four gaps or gates as shown in the diagram, and with a large flat stone in the middle. Each player moved his 'man'—another stone— a space at a time right round the ring, leaving at the same gap through which he entered. To land on one of the other gaps usually involved some punishment such as returning to the start or waiting, and the moves were regulated by the throw of three pieces of cane split in half so that one side of each was flat and the other rounded. These staves were thrown on the flat central stone together, and when they came to rest the score was counted by such rules as: all rounded sides up, 10 spaces; two rounds up, 3; no round up, 5. Variations of this game were widely played, and some boards were marked on skins so that they were always available.

But the real story of recreation does not start until the arrival of the settlers in the seventeenth century. For these there was no relaxation: for one thing, the very reason that many of them had fled from Europe was that they regarded pleasure as sinful, and they were hardly likely to change their strict Puritan views in the weeks of the crossing, however uncomfortable it might have been. Yet even if they had wanted to indulge in a life of gaiety they would have had little chance for the colonists in southern states, whose religion did not force them to frown on pleasure, had no more leisure than the most devout Puritan in New England.

Like their Saxon ancestors over a thousand years before, they had to clear the forest, till the soil, build homes and barns, all in the rare intervals between the almost ceaseless battles against wild men, wild animals, and wild nature. There was no time for leisure in the new

Indians at play

land, and wise governors made virtue out of necessity. Jamestown, for instance, sentenced any tradesman not properly attending to his work every day to three years in the galleys. All games were naturally banned in most states, and actors and theatrical performances were singled out for the most violent attacks. Massachusetts even forbade 'unnecessary' walking in the streets and fields on Sundays, the only time free from the back-breaking day-long toil. Smoking and drinking were firmly regulated, and clothes had to be of the plainest styles and drabbest materials, so that no secret fun could be obtained from this source.

When in the middle of the seventeenth century a midweek religious meeting called The Great and Thursday was introduced many of the church leaders who realized that it was attended more for social reasons than for pious ones were faced with a problem. They knew it was a sly way round the prohibition on pleasure, yet they could hardly forbid the people to attend their place of worship. Neither could the elders find an excuse for stopping fishing or shooting as these were sheer necessities of life, but no doubt they warned their congregations that to enjoy the hunt was wicked, even if it had to be done to keep the family alive. Nevertheless almost every colonist must have indulged in what were really the only permitted pastimes, and so Fishing in particular, America's No. 1 pastime to-day, got off to a sound start.

As the years passed and the eastern seaboard became cleared and settled, and more and more colonists who were not Puritans crossed the ocean, it became increasingly difficult to hold the settlers against their wills. The stern old leaders had done a wonderful and indispensable job, but the need for their savage severity had passed away. There were constant skirmishes between the authorities and the men and women who with great ingenuity created and invented some form of relaxation, which was so essential as a relief from their hard lives.

Much though the elders may have disliked it, they had to permit taverns to be built for the benefit of travellers and traders. With other amusements so hard to come by, it is no wonder that many people unfortunately turned to drinking as their chief pastime. As rum cost only about sixpence (seven cents at modern rates) a quart, it is not surprising that the authorities soon had the problem of drunkenness to add to their other woes.

As the years rolled on towards the eighteenth century the southern states, now well established and colonized in the main by pleasure-loving people, began to enjoy themselves as the slaves took over more and more of the labour. Even the stern New England states had to give way little by little, but the Puritan influence remained to restrict too much freedom.

The eighteenth century itself was, with perhaps the exception of the troubled decades of the wars against the French and the British, the Golden Age of American recreation. Work was still hard, dangerous, and lengthy, especially as the pioneers pushed the frontiers back and back, but the folk entered into their pastimes with the same full-blooded zest that they did their labours.

The towns were still fairly small, and by far the biggest proportion of the population lived in the countryside so that nearly all of the recreation was of a rural kind, growing wilder and wilder as one pushed farther into the unexplored west.

In the south Horse-racing was the traditional sport, and though legally it was confined to 'gentlemen,' it was impossible in states where almost every one had a horse to enforce this rule. The fields were there, the spare time, and the gambling spirit, so Horse-racing was inevitable.

Cockfighting too had a terrific hold on the plantations, masters, slaves, and poor whites huddling round a tiny ring to wager on the result of the battle between the vicious little birds. Boxing, a duel very similar in its savagery to the cockfight except that the combatants were much bigger, also attracted a large following, and foreign visitors were constantly complaining that Virginia and the Carolinas seemed to do nothing but indulge in these three pastimes.

But this was not entirely true, and if the traveller had gone to the quieter parts he would probably have found the south enjoying very similar recreations to the north, and most of these were connected with the home and family.

In all parts of America every stage in the setting up of a new homestead was the excuse for a day's fun—Log-rolling, House- and Barn-raising, Quilting, and Husking. The new settler would fell the trees in his clearing and on the day appointed neighbouring farmers and their families would ride over to help in moving the heavy baulks of timber—a task which would not take long. The rest of the day was given to merry-making, feasting, drinking, and dancing. Later on, when the house or barn was ready to be erected, there was another gathering for assistance and fun.

When the home was ready the womenfolk would hold parties to make the tedious patchwork quilts, and this time it was the men who came merely to enjoy themselves. And finally there were the annual Husking-bees when the whole neighbourhood met at one barn after another to husk the corn and indulge in a riot of merriment. The highlight for many of this last operation was the discovery of a red ear which entitled the man who found it to a kiss from any girl of his choice in the company.

When the working part of the day had ended the fun began with a huge meal, and plenty of drink, both home-made and bought. Story-telling, Dicing, Shuffleboard, or Card-playing might follow; parlour games in which all could join—I love my Love with an A, and all the old favourites—would most probably make an appearance, and when the evening got warmed up Dancing was certain. Reels, jigs, folk-dances and made-up dances made the floor shake as the merrymakers, getting hotter, redder, more excited, and more drunk, pounded away the hours of the night. Usually there was some one who could play a fiddle, but if no one had the skill it mattered little for the dancers sang the tune themselves as they whirled round.

Weddings, christenings, and funerals all provided an excuse for social family gatherings, though on the more solemn of these occasions perhaps the dancing time which would hardly have been respectable was given over to eating and drinking.

As districts became more settled there were rare days of public holiday to add to the private ones: elections and gatherings of the militia for training brought together crowds of people, often from long distances. With the duties which had brought them together completed as quickly as possible, every one surrendered himself to the holiday mood. There would be organized entertainments such as Bull- or Bear-baiting with dogs (particularly in the south), chasing a greased pig, Horse-racing, Trotting-races, Foot-races, Jumping, Dancing and Fiddling competitions, Cudgel and Sword duels, Ninepins, Bowls, and in places where the English were strong, Cricket, though this was rather too slow for most. For the more violent there was a wild Football with no rules, no limits, and plenty of injuries, and an even more savage Wrestling. Here again there were few rules, the practice of trying to gouge out one's opponent's eyes with the thumbs being considered excellent sport in some states.

Pitching the horse-shoe at a stake was an outlet for the more elderly men but there must have been few who did not join the shooting at

Goose-pulling

tethered bears and turkeys. When the excitement of the games and perhaps the travelling fair and sideshows had been exhausted there was sure to be Dancing, often all night.

Farther west on the frontier where life was harder and rougher the fun was correspondingly more violent. Here the gun and a man's own strength and skill were the means whereby he clung to life, and it is not surprising that these were the things he loved to show off when he met his fellows. The disregard for life—or perhaps tremendous skill in aiming —is reflected in the fact that one of the favourite sports was to shoot at a tin mug balanced on a man's head at forty paces, the winner receiving a quart of whisky. Most probably the man holding the target, if still alive, needed more than that to restore his nerves to their proper state.

Perhaps only the best marksmen survived to take part in these meetings, but the skill of those who did seems uncanny. A nail was often tapped into a tree or post, and then the competitors tried to drive it home by hitting it on the head with bullets. One shot in three was said to strike the nail fair and square, and at forty paces again this was no mean shooting. At other times the target was a lighted candle taken into the woods after dark, the object being to cut off the end of the wick at fifty yards without putting out the flame. In all of these contests, of course, heavy gambling was a major part of the amusement.

When the shooting had ended there would be weight-lifting, hurling logs of wood, fights with tomahawks (a trick learned from the Indians), brutal wrestling-matches, and general racing and jumping. The savagery of the time and place is shown by the popularity of Goose-pulling, in which an unfortunate goose was hung upside down by a rope from the branch of a tree. Each man in turn galloped on his horse underneath, and grabbed at the creature's head, which had been well greased, to try to pull it off. The one who succeeded had the carcass, and a second victim was strung up. Though such pastimes seem so cruel, we can hardly expect men who were daily risking their own lives to be squeamish about those of wild animals.

So thoroughly had Dancing permeated the American nation that even in the wild frontier it was an essential part of any entertainment. Women were naturally very scarce so that if local conditions permitted Indian squaws were welcomed as partners. If the local tribe were not the best of friends half of the men might be designated 'women' and

Early Golf

distinguished by a handkerchief or coloured band tied round the arm.

Sometimes there would be shooting-parties in which each animal was allocated a number of points, say, a rabbit five, and a deer five hundred. At the end of the day each group of hunters would add up its score, and the losers gave a feast to the rest. Then, weary and full, but still thirsty, the men would fall back on sports which never failed—telling tales, singing, and attending to their guns.

Boasts of shooting prowess and the size of animals they had caught were bandied to and fro across the fire, and sooner or later a story of one or other of the frontier heroes was bound to make its appearance. Daniel Boone, Mike Fink, Davy Crockett, and Paul Bunyan at every retelling grew bigger, stronger, braver, more skilful, and more like the gods of old. The grizzled, hardened veterans, still children at heart, never failed to delight in the stories of the men who were their idols.

Back on the Atlantic fringes the towns, though still tiny by modern standards, were growing, but because of their closeness in spirit, if not in distance, to Europe, had not the distinctive character of the true American countryside. Their amusements were still very much those of the parts of the Old World from which they had sprung: the nobility had their horse-races, balls, assemblies, concerts, and hunting. Billiards flourished, and occasionally a 'real' tennis-court might be seen in the 'English' areas, while the French had their carnivals, and the Dutch skated and played Golf. This was not the immensely popular game of the twentieth century but a kind of cross between Miniature Golf and an outdoor Bagatelle played in a small pen rather like a sheepfold. Sleighing, which was something of a novelty for those from Western Europe, became very popular indeed, with racing and pleasure drives in private and public sleighs.

In the middle of the eighteenth century Cricket was fairly wide-spread, while travelling acrobatics or showmen with freaks and outlandish animals in cages became more common in the larger towns. Theatres too appeared, New York having one as early as 1699, but the high prices of the seats ensured that they were on the whole an entertainment for the wealthy. The actors were almost entirely English companies who gave performances of Shakespeare and the current shows of the London stage. In the 1770's, when relations between the colonies and the Government in England became strained, most of the theatres closed, and when after Independence they were free to re-open the bitterness against anything connected with the British was so strong that drama remained dead for almost another twenty-five years.

The most American of the town recreations was Ninepins, which, although played in England, never had quite the following that it had across the Atlantic, and Trotting which surprisingly had no parallel in Europe. Beginning with friendly challenges as gentry and farmers trotted along the roads in their light carriages to town, Trotting caught the imagination of the public, and before the end of the century tracks were springing up in every settlement of any size. Even when staged on a proper course the light-carriage-races kept much of their earlier friendliness and freedom from the rowdyism that went with ordinary Horse-racing. Therein lay much of their charm.

For ten years the colonists' minds turned to thoughts more serious than recreation, and even when the last angry shot had been fired and the last inky word had dried on the peace treaty the new nation found it could not quite return to the old free-and-easy ways of pleasure. The new boy in the world's school had to show his older classmates that he was a power to be considered, a figure of importance. For the first forty or fifty years of the nineteenth century the average American returned to something like the spirit of his founding forefathers two hundred years earlier. Work! Work! Work! was the symbol of the new republic, though the struggle was not now for the life of each individual but for that of the state. A fever of love of gold and power too swept the land so that those who did not toil for patriotic motives did so from selfish ones.

If these reasons were not enough a new religious fervour took hold of the country in the shape of revival meetings in which the old Puritan ideals of labour were strong. Work for its own sake was godliness, and leisure and recreation were automatically sin—or so thundered the preachers from a thousand platforms to huge congregations half dazed by the mass singing of rousing hymns.

But whether from motives of good or evil, the first fact that impressed foreign visitors to the United States in the first decades of the nineteenth century was the pale faces, the weary eyes, the rounded shoulders, and unhealthy bearing of the workers shuffling from factory and office to their beds.

In the country areas, and in the south, now in its heyday of the slave era, things were a little better, and the traditional games and pastimes continued, if on a reduced scale, for the grim-eyed devotion to the 'mighty dollar' had taken a grip even there.

If the ordinary man did seek recreation he was usually too exhausted mentally and physically to make any efforts to entertain himself. Unlike his forefathers who had made everything for themselves, including their pastimes, the new townsman bought his food, clothing, and housing, and expected to buy his amusement so that he did not have to exert himself at all. Yet for the decent citizen even if he had money to spare, there was little enough to buy. Entertainment was largely confined to the wealthy few who could afford their concerts, assemblies, and balls in private, and to the dregs of humanity whose income and leisure alike was most suspicious. Until half-way through the nineteenth century the average American in the towns seemed to have suddenly lost his zest for vigorous independent life. When his work had ended he had little choice of amusement: the brawling, noisy inn, the bowling-alley, and billiard-saloon, with their vice and wickedness; the coarse, low dens called theatres, and an occasional illegal murderous boxing-match, competed with a rare circus or menagerie and the revival meeting.

The taverns as always offered Dicing, Card-playing, and Shovelboard to relieve the weary workman of his wages, and as innkeepers boasted openly that a man could get drunk twice for sixpence (seven cents) the sharpers were always active. In the bowling-alleys the professional gamblers and tricksters reached such a state that Connecticut and New York states made Ninepins illegal. But the law caused scarcely a momentary pause among the gamblers, for the proprietors of the alleys merely added a tenth pin and re-arranged them in a triangular formation instead of the usual diamond. As the century advanced Bowling gained respectability, especially when in 1895 the American Bowling Congress was formed to regulate the game. To-day it ranks second only to Angling in the number of enthusiasts it claims.

Drama reached its lowest ebb in the nineteenth century for as soon as the theatres began to re-open in the big cities about 1800 they attracted the roughest and worst elements of society. Prices of admission ranged from 12 to 50 cents, and drunken, shirtsleeved, shouting, sweating ruffians jostled on the hard, often backless, benches, chewing and fighting, to watch performances which became more and more depraved. The unheated, rat-ridden, stinking, and rotten buildings were frequently death-traps for the crude candle, oil, or gas lighting caused many fires often with loss of life. The Bowery alone was burned down four times in seventeen years. It is not surprising that the middle and upper classes stayed away from the theatres except those few which by charging higher prices managed to keep some semblance of order. It is not surprising too that the rabble soon threw out Shakespeare and other serious plays in favour of melodrama, the coarser the better. Stages were filled with the continuous roar of six-shooters, the scream of 'dying' Indians, and the hullaballoo of saloon brawls as Western after Western occupied the boards. Occasionally novels adapted for the stage in the broadest and most blatantly sentimental form were shown—*Uncle Tom's Cabin*, before the Civil War, had runs which would make a twentieth-century producer green with envy.

In provincial towns where huge theatres began to be built in the thirties and forties things were even worse. The travelling troupes of actors were often tenth-rate, and more often than not drunk long before the performance began. They rarely knew their parts but improvised as far as their fuddled brains would allow. Only the main characters moved from town to town playing in barns, halls, and theatres as the supers were engaged locally. Many of these were paid largely in whisky, and no great standard was expected—or obtained. Once, when a party of Indians were engaged for a crowd scene, they drank their wages beforehand so that they went berserk on the stage. The whole stage was wrecked before the inflamed extras could be quietened down.

Soon after the middle of the century rowdiness and violence on the stage turned to nastiness as burlesque swept the country. The roaring drunken actor was replaced by girls whose singing and dancing appealed to an even lower type of audience. Legitimate drama was a feeble, struggling light, and yet the native decency struggled to reassert itself.

Not all was black: for the highbrows the New York Philharmonic Orchestra was formed in 1842, and opera had its first real home in the New World when the Metropolitan Opera House was opened in 1883. For those whose tastes were just a little lower the Gilbert and Sullivan light operas swept the land as soon as they were performed and for the great mass of homely folk to whom the higher flights did not appeal those two great American institutions, vaudeville and the minstrel show, put in their appearance about the middle of the century.

Vaudeville, with its succession of turns of comedians, acrobats, singers, jugglers, conjurers, and performing animals, could fit into any society: if the place demanded it it could be every bit as crude as the burlesque, but usually it was good, clean fun, and entertainment for the family. The nigger minstrels, which reached their peak in the 1840's and 1850's, filled a great need in American society—the decent workman and the middle-class families could enjoy a harmless evening's recreation with the painted clowns and their quick-fire patter, their topical jokes, their dancing, and above all the nostalgic songs of Stephen Foster. When, however, the Civil War revealed the true state of things in "de south" the sentiment melted in the harsh light of anger, and the minstrels suffered a blow from which they never recovered.

For the respectable man whose principles barred him from theatre, tavern, and gambling-hall there was little left. Some found relief in the emotional religious meetings, and many, more quietly, in the wave of self-education that swept the country. Eager machine-minders and office-workers thronged the public halls late in the evening to listen to travelling lecturers opening the doors to what must be admitted were often very dusty corridors of information. Astronomy, geology, philosophy, and a score of other subjects helped the better citizens to realize that there was something else in life beside the drudgery of toil, and to cater for the new interest in the outside world, exhibitions of curios began to open here and there. Some were the public museums opened by the towns themselves, but more often they were commercial shows, the most famous, of course, being that of Phineas T. Barnum whose permanent museum in New York contained a picture-gallery, working models, a zoo, wax-works, and a whole collection of freaks, some genuine, others the products of the man's amazing genius.

But Barnum, despite his immense field of activity—concerts—including the unprecedented Jenny Lind series—lectures, museums, animal shows, and later, circuses—could amuse only a minute fraction of the population. Most of the remainder plodded through their grey lives bounded by dog-weary sleep and monotonous toil.

Yet in the 1840's came the first real sign that there were better things in store. Starting as a small trickle, and growing rapidly broader towards the end of the decade as floods of German refugees poured into the country from the political upheavals of Europe, came the gymnasia. Here amid the dumb-bells, Indian clubs, parallel bars and ropes, the pale cheeks of a swelling crowd of men and women began to take on a healthy pink glow that was to be symbolic of the change in the outlook of the American towndweller in the next half of the century.

A new spirit seemed to enter the land after 1850. The dollar was still a mighty attraction, but the nation as a whole felt that it had made itself a power to be considered in the councils of the world. As two generations of grim, unremitting toil in the seventeenth century had brought the tiny, struggling colonies to a state of relative security where they might spare an hour for leisure, so it was nearly two hundred years later with the great republic. For the next forty years America threw herself into recreation with that same enthusiasm and energy that had characterized her work for the previous fifty. Sports of every description flourished, and the nation kicked, hit, pulled, pushed, walked, ran, hurled, or pedalled its vigorous way through its leisure hours. But, alas, in some quarters the great upsurge of energy was showing signs of burning itself out before the end of the century, for in the last two decades spectator sports began really to make themselves felt.

The traditional American pastimes of Hunting, Shooting, and above all Fishing, which had almost everywhere passed from the realm of necessity into that of pleasure, went from strength to strength. The countryman had never once ceased to enjoy them, but from about 1870 onward annual holidays became the general custom, and the city worker turned again to the pursuits of his forefathers in woods and by the lakeside. For the ambitious huntsman there were the countless thousands of buffalo roaming wild, and these were mercilessly slaughtered so that before the end of the century they were almost extinct. But for the ordinary man there were plenty of ordinary creatures to shoot in forests which the constantly spreading railroad brought within easy galloping distance of the most saddle-shy.

Nevertheless for the city worker the field sports were still greedy of time, and the American even in the nineteenth century had little enough to spare. Many preferred their exercise in short violent bursts, and this helped the national game of baseball in the 1840's to emerge from its mysterious and debatable origins.

To hit a ball with a club is almost instinctive, and there had of course been many traditional children's games which bore a strong resemblance to Baseball—in America the most common were called One- (Two-, Three-, or even Four-) Old Cat, and in England Rounders. But it is surprising to see in a list of pastimes in a children's book printed in London, in 1744, entitled *A Little Pretty Pocket Book* one definitely called Baseball. In the picture, which shows only part of the pitch, a striker, a pitcher, a catcher, and at least two bases are clearly displayed. How many bases there were, or how many players took part in the eighteenth-century game, is not known, for unfortunately no description is included.

The rules and positions in the early games, however, were most probably made up locally to suit the players and the pitch, but one fundamental difference seems to have been that the batter could be out by being hit by a thrown ball. This of course meant that the ball had to be a soft woollen or cotton one, with all the restrictions that implied on distance of hitting and bouncing.

This was probably the game which Doubleday played and certainly popularized in the early years of the nineteenth century. While he did little to make the rules, the necessity for these was felt only when Abner's enthusiasm and gospelling had set the sport on its nationwide rocketing to fame. The lack of uniformity and the limitations of the soft ball were being acutely felt by the 1840's when matches between one district and another were being played, so that in 1845 the Knickerbocker Club under Alexander Cartwright laid down what were almost the modern rules. The all-important tagging rule, instead of throwing, soon led to the introduction of a hard ball and a general improvement in performance. Since then changes have been relatively small, and brought about as techniques by the various players improved—at times the batter was on top and sometimes the pitcher, and means had to be found to keep a balance by restricting some aspects of the game or by giving more freedom to others.

The aristocratic Knickerbockers tried hard to keep 'their' game for the upper class, but with the only requirements a stick, a ball, and a relatively small patch of open ground there was no holding it. By 1860 there were scores of clubs of ordinary men with dozens more being formed weekly up and down the land: the game had arrived.

Football, Baseball's only possible rival as a team game, had a chequered career, but from the start its roughness, its complicated rules, and the fact that it is limited to the youthful and virile hindered its progress. Most of the colleges had from their beginnings played their own variations of the age-old 'football' games, but as the rules were so different there could be little challenging. In 1867 a start was made when a Princeton twenty-five-man team played a match of sorts against twenty-five from the Theological Seminary, but soon the first major quarrel was to develop when Harvard, where Football had been banned until 1872, adopted the English Rugby, or carrying game, while the other universities continued with their kicking one.

Four years later Yale, Rutgers, Princeton, and Columbia decided that Harvard had been right after all, and adopted the 'Rugby' style. But Harvard was still out of step and demanded an eleven-man team, while the remainder kept theirs at fifteen. The game spread rapidly, affording an outlet for speed and skill, and all the while experimenting went on with the rules which were altered by general consent when thought fit.

In 1888, however, a bad move was made when knee-high tackling was permitted, for at once the game became dominated by sheer brute force instead of fleetness and cunning. At the same time new tactics were introduced to exploit the new heavyweights, and Football became almost as brutal and as full of injuries as its savage medieval forerunners. In addition, the colleges fell to quarrelling among themselves, and the general public were loud in their criticisms of the whole business.

At length the tumult reached such a pitch that in 1905 President Roosevelt summoned the representatives of the major universities interested to the White House. As a result of the President's drastic step the National College Athletic Association was formed which set to work to evolve the modern sport.

Less spectacular, perhaps, but drawing a far greater number of participants than the major ball games were the lesser sports. Cycling, for example, hit America like a whirlwind in the 1860's, seventies, and eighties, so that it must have seemed to one living then that every human creature was hurtling up and down the dusty roads on Penny-farthings or on safety-cycles. Women too thronged to take up the new craze, which did a great deal for the health of the nation as a whole, enabling them to get cheaply and pleasantly into the clean air of the countryside. Working America stampeded to the bicycle as it did to the automobile and television in the next century.

The only pastime ever to approach Cycling in numbers was Roller-skating, which was also an import from Europe. From about 1870–80 every town that prided itself on its status had its rink, and, as in England, millions spent every free moment in a harmless, healthy, if rather noisy, pastime hurtling round and round the concrete or asphalt rink.

Croquet and Archery enjoyed for a quarter of a century a wave of popularity, but their appeal was confined largely to the wealthy classes and those who sought to enter the ranks of society. The fashionable set had been driven from the sole possession of one sport after another by the virile democracy, and clung to these games, which did not attract the average citizen, as symbols of their 'apartness.'

Tennis too was introduced from England to Nahant, Boston, in 1874, and to Newport, R.I., a year later. Dr James Dwight, F. R. Sears, and the Outerbridge family were among the earliest enthusiasts of the new 'society' game, but although the first lawn tennis club was organized by the Staten Island Cricket and Baseball Club as early as 1875, no one took the game very seriously, any racquet, ball, net, rules, or dress being used to suit the occasion. The burly male looked down his nose at the gentle pat-patting, and if he condescended to play at all he did not bother to remove top-hat, jacket, or heavy boots.

Gradually, however, the magic of the game caught him: there was more to it than he had thought, and lighter, more suitable clothing was hastily adopted as skill and speeds increased. Such a hold did the new pastime take that the United States National Lawn Tennis Association was formed in 1881 to lay down the laws of the game and generally to supervise its running. In 1900, only a quarter of a century after its feeble, effeminate beginnings, Tennis reached the standard of an international sport when Dwight F. Davis gave his cup for the championship of the world—an award which was fittingly won for the first time by the United States.

Golf, surprisingly, got off to a very unpromising start when the first real course (as opposed to the miniature course of the Dutch) was opened at Yonkers, in 1888. The old-fashioned leather ball stuffed with feathers was most unsatisfactory when it became waterlogged and heavy, and the peculiar red coat which it was customary to wear when playing immediately labelled one as 'peculiar.'

The gutta-percha ball, introduced towards the end of the century, made the game much more accurate and skilful, and the new sport gradually gained ground though it was not until the early 1920's that the craze really burst. As late as 1914 there were still only two hundred courses in the whole of the United States. Fifteen years later half of all

Roller-skating

the golf-courses in the world were in North America. The townsman in particular found that Golf offered him just the combination of exercise and complete mental relaxation that his high-pressure life demanded, with the result that, with Angling and Bowling, it has become one of the top three participant sports to-day.

So far America had yet to invent a popular sport all of her own: she had borrowed, changed, adapted, and altered, but the time was fast approaching when she would give to the world a brand new game in the shape of Basketball. James Naismith, coach at Springfield Y.M.C.A., stared at the hard, frozen ground in winter and then back to his bored ball players, waxing flabby in the cold months. Realizing the need for a fast, light game to keep his men in trim, he experimented with a large light ball and two fruit-baskets on the end walls of his gym. Immediately his new game caught on and spread far beyond Massachusetts, for the world saw how easily it could be adapted to old or young, highly trained or mere beginner, outdoors or in.

But amid the welter of sports that flourished there began to grow a more disturbing element—the passive spectator. While there had always been entertainments such as Horse-racing, Trotting, the theatre, and circus in which the ordinary person could not take part and which were designed to be watched by others, many people in the latter quarter of the nineteenth century, quite able to play themselves, found that they preferred to sit looking at others, and particularly at those more highly skilled. This in turn led to a new development inside the games themselves—the emergence of the professional, the man who played because he was paid to do so, not always because he entirely enjoyed it. The full-time professional, besides usually having more natural skill, obviously spent all of his time practising, which in turn gave him yet more skill, so that the gulf between the amateur, who played for fun when he had a spare hour, and the professional grew steadily wider. As early as 1869 the first all-professional Baseball team, the Red Sox, went on tour, and not unnaturally were unbeaten. The full-time team had arrived on the scene, and with it, unfortunately, gambling, the ballyhoo of commercialism, and the shady figures that occasionally do not recognize the line between legality and sharp practice.

The combat between two highly trained skilful teams set the seal on the popularity of Baseball as a spectator sport though fortunately for every league match played there must be countless thousands of spare patch games between scratch teams who keep the old spirit alive.

Football from its very beginning had to be a game for the majority to watch, for the qualities of youth, speed, strength, skill, and courage are combined in very few of the general population. Ice-hockey, introduced in the last years of the century, for similar reasons could never become widespread as a sport for the ordinary man to take part in.

Although Tennis and Golf both have developed professionals since the nineteenth century, the process has not gone as far as it has with the major ball games, and they still are mainly games to be played by the enthusiastic amateur. Their very nature tends to limit the commercial and spectator aspect, for the small size of the tennis-court means that only a relatively small crowd can watch compared with that at a baseball- or football-match. As the main object of the spectators is to sit in comfort, and be entertained, few of them take kindly to Golf, in which the watcher has to exert almost as much energy as the player himself, wandering round the long processions of fairways and greens.

Perhaps the most commercialized and most completely spectator sport of all is Boxing, and quite understandably too, for even fewer people have the skill and inclination to enter the ring than the football-field.

For most of the nineteenth century Boxing in America was a bloodthirsty, barefisted mauling, fought under Broughton's London Prize Ring Rules (no timed rounds, no time-limit to the match, bare fists). Officially the 'sport' was illegal, but 'championship' bouts took place in well-known 'secret' rendezvous, and the results were widely discussed in the papers. Even so, the average citizen took little interest in the savagery, and few realized that when J. L. Sullivan defeated Jake Kilrain in 1889 for the doubtful title of Champion of America that the last major contest under the old Prize Ring Rules had been fought. A year or so later, some thirty years after they had been adopted in England, the Marquess of Queensberry rules were adopted. These, with their insistence on three-minute rounds and padded gloves, at once put Boxing on a new footing, though for a year or two, until the public realized the change, fighting did not gain wide respect. It was left to Jim Corbett, who beat Sullivan in the first glove championship in 1892, finally to set the sport on its climb to fame.

The greatest ally of the commercial sports was perhaps the advance of technology, especially where it was concerned with transport. Railroad and river-steamers scurried the crowds to games which would have been far beyond their reach in the days of the horse and carriage. Soon mechanization, no longer content to be a minor partner, began to set up in business as an entertainer in its own right, and in the last decade of the nineteenth century the electric trolley became a major relaxation of the townsman. On Sundays and holidays thousands would board the brightly lit, decorated vehicles, which were often complete with resident brass band, and rumble away on a tour of the neighbourhood. Often instead of an idle tour the trolleys made for near-by seaside beaches which were just coming into fashion, but more frequently the terminus was a pleasure-park built just outside the town itself. Here the pleasure-seekers, disgorged from their gaudy transports, could merely sit in pleasant surroundings or else enter the expensive whirl of amusements provided to drain their pockets and fill those of others. Steam-powered merry-go-rounds with blaring organs, helter-skelters, roller-coasters, Ferris-wheels, and sideshows brought the old-fashioned fair up to date, while for the millions to whom Dancing was still the great entertainment a garishly decorated hall was provided. Saloons, eating-houses, and trinket-stalls completed the still familiar scene.

For a few years the trolley-madness swept the country, but one small sideshow in the parks on which they vomited their hordes had rung the death-knell of not only the lurching electric tram but also many other forms of recreation. From about 1890 Edison's invention, the kinetoscope, began to appear in fairs and arcades as a successor to the old-fashioned peepshow. For a nickel in the slot the customer peered into a tall boxlike machine and saw for less than sixty seconds a flickering, moving picture. A simple action such as a man sneezing or a person walking across a room delighted the unsophisticated viewers as the infant cinema burst upon America.

While the craze lasted the arcade proprietors rolled in their profits, for no one expected the boom to last long. But the prophets had not bargained with the inventors. Just as the first enthusiasm was dying away they succeeded, in 1894, in projecting a moving picture on a screen. Now groups of people could watch at once, but even then the first dim two-minute reels in the narrow nickelodeons gave no real hint of the greatness to come.

For nine years the cinema seemed to stand still, as if gathering itself for the next great step—one which to us now is so obvious. In 1903, for

An electric trolley-car

the first time, a real story was told in moving pictures, and though *The Great Train Robbery* lasted but a brief twelve minutes, it settled all doubts: the greatest spectator recreation of all time up to that date had been born, and merely awaited the terrific exploitation it was to receive in the next decades.

Before the century had finally died there were other hints abroad on how the Americans of the next fifty years would amuse themselves, though few perhaps guessed exactly how far and how fast developments would take place. The rare clanking automobile of the 1890's, crawling at fifteen miles an hour between its frequent breakdowns, did not forecast the millions of hurtling gleaming monsters of the twentieth century. Nor did the wheezy scratching of Edison's early phonograph really prepare the future for the welter of Hi Fi stereophony and Top Tens of the 1960's. Even less did those who were privileged to see scientists and electricians pottering over their almost completed apparatus visualize the tidal wave of radio and television that was to threaten the whole structure of recreation.

The story of our present century is soon told: more and more man has sought 'easy' recreation; more and more has the task of amusing the nation fallen into the hands of big business. Overpowering 'crazes' have come, and been dead within a year or so—the yo-yo, Miniature Golf, and the peculiar dances, to name only a few. The cinema on its dizzy pinnacle in the 1930's seemed as though it would dominate the world of leisure for ever, yet within a few years it was gasping before the savage blows of television.

Recreation, like so much else in life, will give dividends only if capital is put in. With the machine taking away so much of the drudgery of existence there is more and more energy and time waiting to be expended. If this is spent solely in passive amusements there is little lasting benefit to anyone.

The old proverb says that if a thing is worth doing it is worth doing well. Might it not be equally true that if a thing is worth doing at all, it is worth doing even badly. We cannot all be first-rate athletes or musicians or painters, and a twentieth-rate performance of one's own is far more valuable than watching the first-rate performances of the world's top-line artistes. Fortunately for the world, youth seems to realize this.

The kinetoscope

Bibliography

General

CARCOPINO, J. (translated by T. Rowell): *Daily Life in Ancient Rome* (Penguin, 1956).

GORDON, L.: *Peepshow into Paradise* (Harrap, 1953).

HARRISON, M., AND WELLS, A. A. M.: *Picture Source Book for Social History* Series (Allen and Unwin).

HARTLEY, D., AND ELLIOT, M. M.: *Life and Work of the People of England* (Batsford, 1931).

LEWIS, C. D. (ED.): *Oxford Junior Encyclopaedia, Volume 9: Recreations* (O.U.P., 1950).

MITCHELL, R. J., AND LEYS, M. D. R.: *A History of the English People* (Longmans, 1950).

POOLE, A. L. (ED.): *Medieval England* (O.U.P., 1958).

QUENNELL, M., AND C. H. B.: *Everyday Things in England* Series (Batsford).

Shakespeare's England (Clarendon Press, 1916).

STRUTT, J.: *The Sports and Pastimes of The People of England*, a new edition much enlarged and corrected by J. C. Cox (Methuen, 1903).

TREVELYAN, G. M.: *Illustrated English Social History*, 4 volumes (Longmans, 1949–52).

TURBERVILLE, A. S. (ED.): *Johnson's England* (O.U.P., 1933).

WYMER, N.: *Sport in England* (Harrap, 1949).

More Difficult Books

ALLEMAGNE, H. R.: *Histoire des jouets* (Paris, 1903).

British Sports and Sportsmen Series (Sports and Sportsmen, Ltd, 1914 onward).

COULTON, G. C. (ED.): *Social Life in Britain from the Conquest to the Reformation* (C.U.P., 1918).

DAREMBERG, C. V., AND SALIO, E.: *Dictionaire des antiquités* (Paris, 1924).

Encyclopédie méthodique dictionaire des jeux (Paris, 1792).

FORBES, R. J.: *Studies in Ancient Technology* (Leiden, 1955–58).

FOSBROOKE, T. D.: *Encyclopaedia of Antiquities* (Nattali, 1843).

FOURQUIERES, B. DE (ED.): *Jeux des anciens, Les* (Paris, 1869).

GILBEY, W.: *Sport in the Olden Time* (Vinton, 1912).

GOMME, A. B.: *Children's Singing Games* (Nutt, 1894).

GOVETT, L. A.: *King's Book of Sports* (Stock, 1890).

Grande encyclopédie des jeux (Paris, 1840).

GULDFORD, E. L.: *Select Extracts illustrating Sports and Pastimes in the Middle Ages* (S.P.C.K., 1920).

HARTOPP, E. C. C.: *Sport in England, Past and Present* (Cox, 1894).

JUSSERAND, J. J.: *English Wayfaring Life in the Middle Ages* (Unwin, 1920).

KIRCHER, R.: *Fair Play: the Games of Merrie England* (Collins, 1929).

LENNARD, R.: *Englishmen at Rest and Play* (O.U.P., 1931).

NETTLESHIP, H., AND SANDYS, J. E.: *Dictionary of Classical Antiquities* (Sonnenschein, 1891).

PIMLOT, J. A. R.: *The Englishman's Holiday* (Faber, 1947).

SALUSBURY-JONES, G. T.: *Street Life in Medieval England* (O.U.P., 1939).

Studies in Medieval History presented to Frederick Maurice Powicke (O.U.P., 1948).

WHITMORE, M. E.: *Medieval English Domestic Life and Amusements in the Works of Chaucer* (Catholic University of America, Washington, 1937).

Indoor Games

AUSTIN, R. G.: Roman Board Games—*Greece and Rome*, Volume 4 (O.U.P., 1934–35).

BENHAM, W. G.: *Playing Cards* (Spring Books, 1957).

FALKENER, E.: *Games, Ancient and Oriental, and How to Play Them* (Longmans, 1892).

MURRAY, H. J. R.: *History of Board Games Other Than Chess* (O.U.P., 1952).

WHITEHOUSE, F.R.B.: *Table Games of Georgian and Victorian Days* (Garnett, 1951).

Sport

ALTHAM, H. S., AND SWANTON, E. W.: *History of Cricket* (Allen and Unwin, 1948).

BERNERS, DAME JULIANA: *Boke of St Albans* (Stock, 1900).

BLAINE, D. P.: *Encyclopaedia of Rural Sports* (Longmans, 1870).

BLOME, R.: *The Gentlemen's Recreation* (London, 1686).

British Sports Series (Batsford).

CRIPPS-DAY, F. H.: *The History of the Tournament in England and in France* (Quaritch, 1918).

DARWIN, B.: *A History of Golf in Britain* (Cassell, 1952).

GARDINER, E. N.: *Athletics of the Ancient World* (O.U.P., 1930).

JACOB, G.: *The Compleat Sportsman* (London, 1718).

JAMES, G. P. R.: *History of Chivalry* (London, 1830).

MARPLES, M.: *History of Football* (Secker and Warburg, 1954).

MARSHALL, J.: *The Annals of Tennis* (London, 1878).

NYREN, J.: *The Young Cricketer's Tutor* (London, 1833).

RADCLIFFE, W.: *Fishing from the Earliest Times* (Murray, 1921).

TWICI, W.: *The Art of Hunting* (Simpkin, 1908).

TURBERVILLE, G.: *The Booke of Faulconrie or Hawking* (London, 1611).
—— *The Noble Art of Venerie or Hunting* (London, 1611).
WOOD, C. A., AND FYFE, F. M.: *The Art of Falconry* (O.U.P., 1955).

Children's Games

BETT, H.: *The Games of Children: their Origin and History* (Methuen, 1929).
DAIKEN, L.: *Children's Toys Throughout the Ages* (Batsford, 1953).
DARTON, F. J. H.: *Children's Books in England* (O.U.P., 1958).
GREENE, V.: *English Dolls Houses* (Batsford, 1955).
GROBER, K.: *Children's Toys of Bygone Days* (Batsford, 1928).
JACKSON, F. N.: *Toys of Other Days* (Newnes, 1908).

Entertainments

CHAMBERS, E. K.: *The Medieval Stage* (O.U.P., 1903).
—— *The Elizabethan Stage* (O.U.P., 1923).
MORLEY, H.: *Memoirs of Bartholomew Fair* (London, 1857).
NICOLL, A.: *The Development of the Theatre* (Harrap, 1948).
WALFORD, C.: *Fairs Past and Present* (Stock, 1883).

Index

Figures in bold type refer to illustrations.